About the Author

.rvived this tragedy and is physically fit and does Tai Chi to
on his co-ordination to become 'Ben' again. However, as a
of the injury he sustained he has some difficulties, such as a poor
term memory, poor hand control and a tremor. But he is enjoy-
e despite these difficulties and setbacks.
ate in his recovery he had a series of head scans. The doctor
'ed showed these, along with scans of another patient, who was
, considerably worse and in a wheelchair, to medical confer-
lelegates. When he asked the audience to predict how the two
ts were doing, they said that he must be in a wheelchair and not
particularly well. At the time, Ben was doing another master's,
: doctor could demonstrate that brain scans were not a very reli-
ndication of the progress people can make after a head injury.
: was this doctor who suggested that Ben write about his expe-
:, as it would give hope to so many other people suffering from
a major trauma. Ben's journey shows that the predictions from
:al staff are not always correct and, given support, one can have
tive and meaningful recovery.

BEN AGAIN

BEN AGAIN

BEN CLENCH

This edition first published in 2017

Unbound

6th Floor Mutual House, 70 Conduit Street, London W1S 2GF

www.unbound.com

ISBN (eBook): 978-1-911586-15-9

ISBN (Paperback): 978-1-911586-12-8

Design by Mecob

Cover image:

© Shutterstock.com / Lightspring
© Shutterstock.com /Krivosheev Vitaly

This book was produced using Pressbooks.com, and PDF rendering was done by PrinceXML.

This book is dedicated to the memory of Jasminder (Jazz) Virdee, to Wirson Correa, and to Dr Santiago Valenzuela Sosa of the Clínica Corazones Unidos, Santo Domingo.

Dear Reader,

The book you are holding came about in a rather different way to most others. It was funded directly by readers through a new website: Unbound.

Unbound is the creation of three writers. We started the company because we believed there had to be a better deal for both writers and readers. On the Unbound website, authors share the ideas for the books they want to write directly with readers. If enough of you support the book by pledging for it in advance, we produce a beautifully bound special subscribers' edition and distribute a regular edition and e-book wherever books are sold, in shops and online.

This new way of publishing is actually a very old idea (Samuel Johnson funded his dictionary this way). We're just using the internet to build each writer a network of patrons. Here, at the back of this book, you'll find the names of all the people who made it happen.

Publishing in this way means readers are no longer just passive consumers of the books they buy, and authors are free to write the books they really want. They get a much fairer return too – half the profits their books generate, rather than a tiny percentage of the cover price.

If you're not yet a subscriber, we hope that you'll want to join our publishing revolution and have your name listed in one of our books in the future. To get you started, here is a £5 discount on your first pledge. Just visit unbound.com, make your pledge and type BENAGAIN in the promo code box when you check out.

Thank you for your support,

Dan, Justin and John
Founders, Unbound

Super Patrons

John Shiell and Jackie Abey
John Allen
James Anderson
India Aspin
FB
Tom Barclay
David Barclay
Robert Barkell
Andrew Barratt
Espen Berg
Julie Blair
Billy Blair
Charlie Blair
Matt Blake
Tom Bowen
James Brown
Jacqueline Burgess
Jacquie Buttriss
Alice Cadogan
Jane Canning
Fiona Carr
Michael Carroll
Caspar Chater
Richard Clarke
Mia Clarke
Jim, Helen and Lindsay Claydon
Theo Clench
Nicholas Clench
Hugh and Jenny Clench
Victoria Clench
Katharine Collins
Diana Conyers
Carrie Cowdry
James Craig
Kim Daborn
Keith Dettmar
Rebecca Dobson

Tom Dobson
Beverly Dobson
Kevin Donabie
Julia Donaldson
Alastair Donaldson
Jerry Donaldson
Ross Downes
Jane Faulkner
George Fereday
Richard Freeman
Vishal Gadhavi
Rob Gordon
Hazel Grice
Yvonne Griffiths
Lloyd Gruber
Simeon Gunn
John Hasson
Jennifer Hasson
Kate Hinchliffe
Robin Hodess
Dominik Horneber
Sharon Hunter
Adam Hussain
Dobrila Ingleby
Izzy Jackman
Andrew Jennings
Dan Kieran
Marina Kobler
Angie Kotler
Eleanor Lamb
Sylvia Lamb
Hilary Lane
Mike Lloyd
Andrew Lord
Keith Lucas
Nicholas Maloney
Marion (Sian's mum)
Glyn and Jane Martin
Liz Mason
Ian and Marg Maynard
Fudgie and Duncan Maynard

Aoife McCullough
Ruth Merttens
Tom Misselbrook
John Mitchinson
Steven Morgan
Kirsty Munro
Mary Needham
Susannah Norman
Peter Norman
Mark Nunn
Michael O'Byrne
Kate Ormond
Jane Osler
Nicky Lloyd Owen
Nigel Padfield
Angela Pell
Jonathan Perry
Simon Phillips
Alison Phillips
Alan Phillips
Justin Pollard
Caroline Radford-Weiss
Adrian Radford-Weiss
Charlotte Randall-Page
Naomi Raybould
Philip Reddaway
Julia Reddaway
Christopher Rose
Jonathen Rose
Lindsey Jane Rousseau
Debbie Russell
Phil Ryan
Harvir Sangha
Ricardo Santos
Sammy Sarfas
Louise Shaxson
Paul Simpson
Jess Smallcombe
Karen Smith
Peter Stafford
Iain Steel

Jim Stephenson
Louise Storey
Verity Susman
Heather Thexton
Christina Thompson
Liz Vivyan
Ali Walmsley
Jacqui Webber-Gant
Oliver Weiss
Linda & Willi
Lizzie Williamson
Wendy Wood
Jenny Young

With grateful thanks to Julia Donaldson, for helping make this book possible.

Contents

Foreword

'Imagine waking up in a place you don't know and where you don't know who you are or why you are there.' This book is the moving story of how Ben came to be in that situation, and how he went on to become 'Ben' again.

I knew Ben's parents, Hugh and Jenny, before he was born, and remember Ben as a lovely and intelligent child, adolescent and young man. So one of the greatest shocks of my life came in an email headed 'Ben and Jazz', in which I read that Ben and his girlfriend had been hit by a car in Santo Domingo, 'killing Jazz instantly and severely injuring Ben.' Through my shock and tears I read on, learning about the 1am hammering on Ben's parents' door by police delivering the news, Hugh's morning flight to San Domingo and the sight of Ben in a coma.

At that stage, when Ben was lying under a dirty, blood-stained sheet in a Third World hospital, there was no certainty that he would ever regain consciousness, and I don't imagine anyone dared dream he would eventually make such an amazing recovery that he would be able to write this book.

Reading Ben's manuscript was an unforgettable experience. It is such a full and honest account, not just by Ben himself but by his family, his friends and some of those who cared for him. Alongside the achievements there are frustrations and setbacks, which are unflinchingly told. But what comes over most strongly is the determination, perseverance and great bravery of Ben's parents – and, above all, of Ben himself.

And what a riveting story it is! Full of suspense, and with fascinating landmarks all along the way, from the moment Ben first opens his eyes: the first smile; the first words; the first awkward movements; the first visit home; the first memories to return. For me one of the most touching early moments is when – in the words of a note kept by his parents when he had been transferred to an English hospital – he 'licked his lips when discussing smoked salmon'.

Ben's physical recovery has been remarkable. Through his hard work and persistence and the dedication of some admirable carers, we see him progress from wobbly bike rides to running an almost incredible half-marathon. And there are plenty of funny incidents in between – notably his indignant diagonal collisions with elderly folk in the swimming pool.

Perhaps even more impressive to me is the mental progress. The brain injury sustained by the car crash affected Ben's memory, concentration and inhibition, and yet in these pages we see him resuming relationships, making new friends and completing an MA course. And, to my mind, the greatest achievement of all has been the planning and writing of this book. I'm sure it will be read and cried, gasped and laughed over by all those who know and love Ben, and by even more people who have never met him. It is a story of tremendous hope and courage.

Julia Donaldson

Abasanjo!

A good example of Ben's slightly confusing remarks early on in his recovery was his use of 'abasanjo'. I think it's now agreed this was his own word for his condition, for the effects of his accident.
Roland Susman, a friend since childhood

*

Ben

I wake and my body isn't working. As I lie here, I can feel things sticking into me. In my arm. In my throat. In my cock.

I sense it's not right but I can't think why. I can't think at all, in fact. Trying to think is too difficult. Confused snippets of thought slip by. They escape me. My mind isn't working. There's a tube up my nose. I try to twitch it. It's uncomfortable. I reach my hand up and tug on the tube. It hurts like hell. I don't know what it is, what it's doing there. I fleetingly sense I don't even know who I am.

Another waking. The confusion is still there. A face looms, close to mine. I want to ask where I am, who I am. I try to say something, but produce small sounds without meaning. The face disappears.

My thinking is all jumbled. Questions surface and sink without real understanding. I feel neither happy nor sad. Emotions and meaning are lost in my confusion, and the confusion only brings anxiety.

Anxiety, I do feel.

Or nothing. Just nothingness.

Then I sleep.

Time passes. I wake often, fleetingly. Each time I feel the confusion and anxiety. Trying to understand is exhausting. It's better I fall asleep again.

A different time. I can hear voices. They tell me to do things: *Push, Ben. Push against me.* A hand is gripping my foot, bending my leg. I try to push. I am responsible for the actions demanded of Ben. But Ben? Who's Ben?

Someone is talking to me with familiar sounds. Different sorts of sounds. I can follow what is being said to me: *Sit up. Look at these pictures. Give me a kiss.* The person, a woman, seems to know me. I try to speak but my voice isn't there. She smiles, encouraging me. The anxiety comes back. I don't know her. I don't know anyone. I still don't know who I am or why I am here.

Hugh, Ben's dad

Saturday, 18 September 2010. I'd had the date in my diary for a long time: it was exactly 40 years since the death of Jimi Hendrix at the tragically early age of 27, and the Handel Society in London were helping to mark the anniversary by vacating their office in Mayfair, the flat Jimi Hendrix lived in during the 1960s, for a three-week period so that its previous layout and furnishings could be restored. As a lifelong Hendrix fan, I'd managed to get two tickets to visit the installation the following week with my son Ben. In the <u>meantime,</u> he was with his girlfriend, Jazz, in the Dominican Republic, where she was enjoying a week's rest and recuperation from her job with the United Nations in Haiti, helping to organise the relief effort after the earthquake the previous January in which more than 220,000 Haitians died.

Ben was due back on Sunday. Early on Saturday I happened to be in the front garden when our daughter Naomi unexpectedly arrived from London to spend the weekend with us. I could see she was upset the moment she walked into the drive. As I greeted her, she broke down in tears. She said she'd woken at about 7am feeling terribly anxious and distressed, and she had no idea why. I consoled her as best I could but she broke down again as soon as she walked through the door and saw Jenny, her mother. Once Naomi had calmed down we discussed whether it was the stresses of her life in London that had caused her upset, and the rest of the day passed without incident.

As I lay in bed that night I was woken at one in the morning by a hammering on the front door. It was unusual, but I guessed that our youngest son Theo, who was out on the town, had lost his key and had been unable to rouse us by the more usual method of using the door knocker.

I opened the door, still barely awake, to be faced by a policeman and a policewoman.

'It's about your son...'

What's Theo been up to? I wondered.

'You have a son who is travelling, sir?'

By this time Naomi had joined me.

'Your son is in the Dominican Republic, sir?'

'Oh, yes... That's my son Ben.'

'I'm afraid there's been an accident, sir, and Ben is in hospital in a critical condition, in a coma. He was hit by a car. Unfortunately, his companion, a young lady, was killed.'

He handed over a piece of paper with the name and number of a Foreign Office official.

'I'm afraid there's not much more we can do to help, sir.'

Jenny was now by my side, and the three of us were in a growing state of partial disbelief. Was this real or a dream? As soon as the police officers left, I rang the number and spoke to someone who was able to confirm Ben was in Dario Contreras Hospital in Santo Domingo.

There was a lady called Lourdes, a Spanish-speaker working for the British Embassy in the Dominican Republic, who could help us.

Within a few minutes I was on the internet looking at flights to Santo Domingo. The first was at 7.30 that morning. In the meantime, Naomi had phoned Theo to tell him the news and he was home within the hour, in a drunken and emotional state. He insisted he accompany me to the Dominican Republic to find his brother. At three in the morning, Jenny was driving us all from our home in Hove to Heathrow Airport, and by 7.30am Theo and I were on our way, via Madrid, where there would be a two-hour wait for the connecting flight.

On arrival at Madrid we learned there was a three-hour delay. We rang to let Jenny and Naomi know. They had meanwhile been in touch with Lourdes, who was sending a driver called Moreno to pick us up at the airport and take us straight to the hospital.

The delay at Madrid made everything feel much worse. What kind of a state was Ben in? A coma surely meant a head injury, which could be life threatening or result in permanent disability. What other injuries did he have? Many was the time I'd admonished him over his sometimes reckless cycling, saying I didn't want to spend the rest of my life pushing him in a wheelchair and wiping his bottom. Was it now coming true? Would I be picking up a body? What would I say at his funeral? Would I be capable of saying anything? These thoughts were endlessly recycled as the hours dragged by. Had Ben taken out any travel insurance? He had discussed whether or not he should do before he went – he was worried about the spate of kidnappings that had recently taken place in Haiti, his first port of call.

There were other concerns. Did we need a visa to enter the Dominican Republic? Would we be able to get out the cash to pay for one on arrival? Neither Theo nor I spoke Spanish. Would we have problems explaining our situation?

As things turned out, the immigration staff seemed singularly disinterested in vetting new arrivals and, after withdrawing money, we were rubber-stamped without question.

Then began the long wait for Moreno, the driver sent by the embassy. We'd finally arrived at around 6.30pm and were standing in the arrivals hall in stifling heat, amid noise and chaos, surrounded by an unfamiliar language and culture. Repeated phone calls meant our mobile batteries were running low, but we established there'd been a mix-up over our arrival time following the delay in Madrid. Lourdes had thought we wouldn't get there until the following day. It felt like the whole situation was unravelling horribly.

Moreno finally appeared at 8.30pm. He spoke very little English and his taxi was a ramshackle affair, but he was clearly sympathetic to our situation and I took to him from the start. However, to add to our existing frustration, we couldn't go straight to the hospital – we had to pick up Lourdes first. Lourdes was short and stout, with her mobile constantly to her ear, translating for us. She exuded an air of efficiency.

At last we arrived at Dario Contreras, the public hospital in Santo Domingo that deals with serious injuries. By now it was about ten o'clock at night and the area outside the hospital was chaos. Crowds of people blocked the drop-off and pick-up point, and there was an armed guard at the door. Ambulances and cars full of distressed relatives and, often, the badly injured seemed to be continuously arriving. There was the constant noise of people milling around and shouting.

Lourdes knew her way through the bustle and walked us straight past a guard who seemed to be engaged in a permanent shouting match with everybody else. We walked along green hospital corridors to the first floor and found the intensive care ward. Lourdes went off to find a doctor while we waited outside. After 45 minutes we were eventually admitted, walking past cramped rows of trauma victims, some conscious, many unconscious, some looking as though they had little chance of survival.

When we got to Ben we couldn't have been met by a more shocking sight. The ward was stiflingly hot and Ben had a single bloodstained sheet pulled half over him. His pillow was covered in blood and sputum, and several tubes had been fed into his lungs to help him breathe, but his breath seemed to be out of sync with the ventilator, making him fight against the machine. An old plastic bottle had been used to try to support his head to stop it falling to one side. His whole body was moving as if he was constantly fitting, and he was drenched in sweat. We later learned that these movements are typical of someone who is decerebrate, when most of the brain is disconnected from the body, leaving only the primitive brainstem to maintain basic functions such as breathing, digestion and a heartbeat.

Ben's left eye was badly bruised – he had obviously been hit very hard on the side of his head, and he had some nasty grazes on his chest and cuts across his stomach, as if a knife had been drawn across it. The index finger of his left hand was bandaged and splinted, and he had some deep gashes in the base of his palm. Thankfully, no bones were broken.

Lourdes arranged an interview with one of Ben's doctors, who explained that Ben had a closed head injury and had not needed surgery. However, his X-rays showed significant swelling to the brain and a lesion on it that was the cause of his decerebrate writhing. Ben was just 27.

There was little more we could do that evening, so Moreno picked us up and took us to the hotel where Ben and Jazz had been staying. We thought this would be the best way of finding out what had happened.

Ben

I still have no clear memory of my trip to Haiti and the Dominican Republic with Jazz, or of the night of the accident. What follows is what I have pieced together from what others have been able to tell me about our plans and movements at that time.

It was September 2010 and I'd been accepted by the Overseas Development Institute (ODI) to spend two years working on the East African Community for the Rwandan government. At the time, Jazz was coming to the end of her contract in Haiti for the UN (United Nations). We were planning for her to join me in Rwanda once she'd finished and I was settled. We hadn't seen each other since June that year, when she came back to the UK for a couple of weeks and we went to the Glastonbury Festival. So before I went off to start my placement, I wanted to spend some time with her. She had two weeks planned for rest and recuperation so we'd arranged that I would first visit her in Haiti, then we would go to the Dominican Republic for a holiday there. Originally she wanted to buy us tickets to Cuba as a treat, but flights to Cuba were too expensive so we decided to hop over the Haitian border to the Dominican Republic at the other end of the island.

During our week in Haiti I met Jazz's friend, Kalinda, who was also working for the UN and was there with her husband Max. In the Dominican Republic, Jazz and I hired a car and drove around visiting beaches, admiring the scenery and enjoying everything the country has to offer.

We were heading back to our hotel after dinner. It was the day before we had to fly back to Haiti, where I'd have to go straight on to the UK to finish up some work before leaving for Rwanda. Our last day. We'd had a relaxing time on the beach before going out to a restaurant close by.

We were walking along the pavement. The pavements in the Dominican Republic are quite high because for some months of the year it rains so heavily that they would otherwise be flooded. It was late at night and as we approached a crossroads in the narrow streets an old saloon car started to cross from one of the side routes. A second vehicle, an SUV (sports utility vehicle), came speeding in our direction, hoping to dash ahead of the saloon, but it didn't make it – instead, it hit the saloon car really hard, which caused the SUV to catapult onto the pavement where we were.

The quiet crossroads in old Santo Domingo where Ben and Jazz were run over

The car knocked me into the street, but it hit Jazz full on. She was killed instantly. I was hit on the side and the car didn't run me over directly, but I was badly injured and needed medical treatment straight away.

Amazingly, there were three doctors in the car ahead of the accident. They heard the crash and stopped to see what had happened. They saw at once that there was no hope for Jazz and that time was critical for saving me, so they drove me straight to hospital themselves. It was the quickest way to get me the medical attention I needed.

These doctors undoubtedly saved my life. One of them, Wirson Correa, even stayed with me through the night to make sure I survived the first few hours after the accident.

I had no broken bones, but I had suffered a major blow to my head, which had damaged both the left and right frontal lobes of my brain. These are the parts of the brain involved in the storing of new memories and the retention of visual memories, processing sensory input, comprehending language, deriving meaning, and for emotions.

Back in the UK I was to have several MRI (magnetic resonance imaging) scans, which showed much more detail than the CT (computed tomography) scans I had in the Dominican Republic. The MRIs showed up what is known as diffuse axonal injury, which is common in people who have had a head trauma. When brain tissue gets violently shaken up, damage can occur to the protective myelin sheaths around some of the neural axons – the part of the neuron that passes messages on to other neurons. The axons form the white matter of the brain and, over time, they die back, cutting off that neuron from sending any outgoing messages. My MRI scans show a random scattering of small voids in my brain where axons had already died back.

For both my dad and my brother to come and find me in such a chaotic place, in such a random part of the world, was amazing, and something I am eternally grateful for. I am so thankful they sprang into action as quickly as they did, and that Theo was there. I think their going together made it easier for each of them to handle the shock of finding me in such an unfamiliar place – and as close as one could come to death without actually dying. I know my dad would have travelled out to get me anyway, but I am pleased Theo could share that burden with him.

I think their determination to help me is part of the reason I did my utmost to recover as best as I could. It made me push myself to do things others wouldn't do to overcome a brain injury. Recovering from this injury hasn't been easy, but I know my struggles have been matched by the extremes of emotion my family have been through. I feel very lucky to have such a family, able to mobilise in minutes to deal so brilliantly with a life-or-death situation on the other side of the world.

Staying Alive

A tale of three hospitals

It's Ben. He will be fine.
He is Ben fucking Fred Clench!
I know he will be fine.
The next morning, when I get to work, I have a picture of Ben
in my hand. I stick it up on the wall at my desk.
I write 'Go, Ben, go' underneath.
Yaz Talebian, a friend since childhood, on hearing the
news of the accident

*

Theo, Ben's brother

Saturday, 18 September 2010. After a normal day at work as a chef in a Brighton restaurant, I went to meet my friends for a few drinks in town. It was just a typical Saturday night, until I got a phone call from my sister at about half past one.

The bar was so crowded I could hardly hear what she was saying. All I heard was, 'Come home! Come home! Jazz is dead.' The phone cut off. I thought I must have heard her wrong.

I went outside to call her again and she said, 'You need to come home, now.'

'What are you talking about?'

Then she uttered a sentence I'll never forget: 'Jazz is dead and Ben might be.'

For some stupid reason I didn't believe her but she said it again. All of a sudden I got a gut-wrenching feeling like I've never had before. I told her I'd be home straight away. I walked back into the bar to find my friends. Tears were streaming down my face. They all asked me what was wrong but I couldn't speak. I finally managed to say the words, 'I think my brother might be dead.' They all stopped still, shocked into silence. I somehow managed to tell them the whole story about where Ben was and what had happened to Jazz.

I wanted to get up and go home but I almost couldn't face it because then I would know it was real. Just as I was getting up to go, my mate Dec came over with a drink and said, 'Theo, you go home and get on that fucking plane with your dad. Don't take no for an answer, make sure you get on that plane and go and get your brother.' He gave me a little slap on the face and again said, 'Go and get on the plane with your dad and look after him and your bro.'

I honestly think it was this little pep talk that made me so insistent when I got back home. I really wasn't going to take no for an answer. I took a cab, and it was the longest cab ride of my life. When I got to the front door I had to sit down outside, smoke a fag and pull myself together. I went inside.

'What took you so long?' said Naomi.

I just said, 'Where's Dad?'

'He's booking flights,' she replied.

I went upstairs to find Dad on the computer. I told him I was coming with him. He said no but I insisted: 'If my brother is about to fucking die, I'm going to get him and I'm not letting you go alone.'

He said no a few more times until I got my point across and we managed to book an early flight.

I remember leaving the house for the airport. All four of us in the car, not really wanting to say anything, just wanting to get to the plane and get going as soon as possible. There was a problem because they wouldn't let us fly without a return ticket. Dad and I tried to explain we didn't know when we would be coming back because of what had happened. The woman at the counter wouldn't listen and made us buy return tickets that cost an arm and a leg. I felt like kicking her head in.

Dad and I just sat there, waiting. The time was going too slowly. We had arrived in Madrid to see our flight to the Dominican Republic had been delayed and we'd have to wait an extra three hours. I thought to myself, *Not on this day. Why does it have to be delayed on this fucking day?* I became certain we were flying out to get his body. We sat in Madrid Airport for what felt like days. I don't think I've ever smoked so many cigarettes.

We didn't say much on the journey. I imagine that in his head Dad was thinking about everything over and over, just like I was, each of us almost forgetting the other was there, just thinking, *Is he alive? Is he dead? What happened? Is Jazz really dead? Is he going to die while we are sitting on this fucking plane? If he has actually died, would we have been there if the plane hadn't been delayed?* I looked over at Dad, who was just staring into space.

The 24 hours of no sleep finally got to me and I nodded off. It felt like just for a second. I woke up and looked at Dad. He had the same expression on his face and was still just staring into space. I'd been asleep for seven hours and I realised he probably hadn't moved that whole time.

We landed in the Dominican Republic, got our bags and went to the arrivals gate, having been told by the Foreign Office that a lady from the British Embassy would be there to meet us. She was nowhere to be seen. We called her and found there had been a misunderstanding about what time we would arrive, due to our delay. She said someone would be there soon. I tried to walk off for a smoke, but Dad asked me where I was going. 'What if she turns up and I can't find you? What if I lose you?' This turned into a little argument, emotions boiling over for both of us. The airport was unbelievably hot and humid, with crowds of people, and lots of shouting. It was chaos, and it all seemed really hostile. Everyone seemed to be staring at us, looking as though they were going to come and mug us or just kick us in. Dad and I were on a knife-edge.

An hour-and-a-half later, after many more cigarettes and many more arguments, this little Dominican man turned up. He didn't speak a word of English, apart from somehow communicating that his name was Moreno and he was going to drive us. We got into his battered taxi and it wouldn't start. I thought to myself, *Here we go, another fucking delay.* Finally he got it running, after realising our bags were blocking the radiator, or the fan – by this time I really didn't care.

We left the airport and drove into Santo Domingo. Even though it was dark, you could tell this place was a shit-hole. Just as I was thinking that, the 'main' road abruptly disappeared and we continued on a mud track that was chock-full of potholes. It was as if no one could be bothered to finish building the road. We arrived at a building somewhere about an hour later and picked up Lourdes, some dumpy little woman from the embassy. She didn't seem to know what was going on, really, just that Ben was in the hospital. She was trying to make small talk like, *Did you have a nice flight?* and stuff, and I had to bite my tongue not to say, *Oh yeah, it was lovely, thanks… What do you think, you stupid bitch? Of course it wasn't! It was hell! The longest hours of my life!*

Eventually we arrived at the hospital. I took one look at the building and thought, *This doesn't look good.* I couldn't help wondering why there was an armed guard on the door. Meanwhile, Lourdes was trying to sort things out with the guard and a man called Claudio. All the time, cars were turning up with people bleeding and looking like they were dying. Mopeds brought in people with broken arms. I was thinking, *Where are the fucking ambulances? This isn't good at all!*

After a lot of explaining and bargaining with the guard we were allowed into the hospital. We went up in the lift to the first floor, where we were told to wait on some little plastic chairs while Claudio went off. About ten minutes later he returned with a young doctor, about five feet tall, with curly ginger hair. He explained in Spanish to Lourdes about what had happened and she attempted to translate. The only words that mattered at this point were that Ben was alive. I can't really remember the rest of the conversation after that. I was just focusing on those two words: 'He's alive.'

At first, the doctor wasn't going to let us go into intensive care to see Ben, because visitors weren't allowed. We explained that we'd been travelling all day and night and we absolutely had to see him. He walked off, saying he'd be back. He was gone for only a few minutes but it felt like hours. He had pulled some strings with the nurses and we were allowed to go and see Ben.

We walked through dimly lit corridors with a few flickering lights. You really wouldn't have known you were in a hospital – it was more like being in a zombie movie or walking through seedy Mafia headquarters. Eventually we stopped at a door. No signs. Nothing. Just a normal door, with frosted glass, that was locked. The doctor knocked on the door, and after a few words in Spanish we were allowed in.

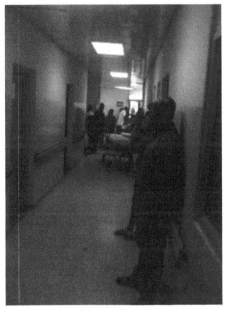

Claudio waiting with us outside the ICU, Santo Domingo, Dominican Republic, September 2010

As soon as we stepped through the door, we were hit by the smell of death – the smell of flesh, blood, brain fluid, piss, shit and all the other things that come out of the human body, all slowly rotting in this room that must have been at least 30 degrees with 90 percent humidity. I looked around and couldn't see Ben. Instead I saw this Dominican guy in a bed right in front of me, sitting up, conscious, with his head wrapped in a bandage and what looked like a clear hosepipe coming out the top of it. There was some sort of fluid streaming out of his skull and down the pipe, into what can only be described as a plastic bucket, the type you take to the beach. I instantly thought, *Fuck, this place is bad.* I'd expected it to be bad, but nothing like this.

We were led along this narrow room towards where Ben was. I scanned every person in every bed as we squeezed down the row, each time looking for my brother. Everyone looked as though they only had about five minutes left in them. There were guys with stab wounds or gunshot wounds. There were guys with half their heads crushed or smashed open, just oozing gunge onto the bed, adding to the layers of congealed blood they'd already been lying in for hours, if not days. All the time the smell was just hitting you in waves. I honestly can't describe it. It's like nothing you could imagine.

We finally got to Ben. He was alive! But he wasn't in a good way at all. There were deep slashes across his chest, half his hand looked as though it had been scooped out with a melon baller and it appeared someone had smashed him in the face with a cricket bat. But he was alive! He was sweating buckets and lying on wet sheets soaked with his sweat and caked with dried blood and mucus, and all sorts of other gunk. He'd been there only 24 hours but it looked as though he'd been there for months, untouched and just left to die, apart from his ventilator.

Dad immediately went to the side of his bed, knelt down, put his hand on his head and said, 'Ben, it's Dad. Theo and I are here to get you. Don't worry, you're safe now.' Ben instantly started writhing around on his bed and his heart rate shot up. Even though he was in a coma and totally unconscious, it was as though he'd heard Dad say those words.

You could tell Ben was extremely uncomfortable. The ventilator was completely out of time with his breathing. Every time he tried to breathe out, it would shoot new air down the pipe into his lungs. I followed the lead coming out of his mouth to a tube with a worn plastic Slinky-shaped thing inside. I followed the tube again and it went straight to an industrial-sized scuba tank. There was no regulator – this thing was so old, it was falling to bits and on a timer. Forcing the air out every few seconds, it was fighting against Ben when it was meant to be keeping him alive.

After only a few minutes, we were asked to leave. I looked at every patient again on the way back, certain most of them would be dead by morning. Dad was in front of me. I paused at the last bed, just for a split second, to look at the guy with the tube coming out of his head. He was in a really bad way. I was surprised he was still alive, let alone conscious. I gave him a little smile. This poor fucker was a dead man. Maybe a smile would make him feel a little better, for a moment. Well, I hoped so. We then stepped outside the door of the 'ward' – I'm not sure you could call it that, it was more like the waiting room for the morgue – and left the hospital.

I looked at Dad. He was so pale. I'd never seen a look on his face like that and I hope I never have to again. We both agreed we needed to get him out of that place as fast as we physically could.

We were driven to the hotel where Ben and Jazz had been staying. The manager met us and he knew who we were straight away. We obviously didn't look like we were there for a holiday. We talked to the staff briefly about what had happened and where the accident had been – just 50 yards from the hotel's front door. One of the ladies who worked there had picked up Ben's bag and put it in his room. We were asked if we wanted to go and see the room and collect their stuff.

The hotel they had chosen was lovely. It would have been a really nice place to stay if the circumstances had been different: an old, Spanish-style building, with archways, set over a couple of floors. Ben's room was directly above our room. We knew we had to find Ben's travel insurance details to get the help he needed. He'd taken out the insurance about two days before travelling, for something like ten pounds. We also needed to collect everything important or valuable – not just documents, laptops and cameras, but things of sentimental value.

A lady from the hotel unlocked the door for us. Jazz's stuff had been collected by the embassy but there was a plastic bag on the floor and the lady from the hotel explained that this was Jazz's too. We gingerly emptied it out onto the bed. It was just clothes, but as we looked through them it became clear these were the clothes she'd been wearing at the time of the accident. They were torn to shreds and covered in blood. I felt physically sick. At that point the fact she was dead really hit home hard. Dad and I looked at each other in silence. I think we were both thinking and feeling the same thing. We folded the clothes up neatly and placed them back in the bag. I will never forget that moment in Ben's and Jazz's room, it will stay with me for the rest of my life.

We took everything we could find down to our room. The manager insisted that we eat and ordered us a Pizza Hut meal and some drinks. I was sitting in the courtyard, using Dad's laptop. Dad was up in our room. We were both crying our eyes out but trying to hide it, trying not to show we were upset, trying to be strong for each other, trying to pretend it wasn't as bad as it was and both simply hoping Ben would still be alive in the morning when we got back to the hospital. I think we could have sat apart all night trying to hide our emotions from each other.

The pizza arrived and the manager put it on the table where I was sitting, along with two beers. I went and got Dad. We were both wiping our eyes and telling each other we were fine. We sat down and agreed Ben couldn't stay in that hospital because he would die within days if he did. We also agreed Mum and Naomi could not, under any circumstances, set foot in there and see the sights we'd seen and the state Ben was in. It would send them into shock, upset them beyond belief. We agreed it wasn't an option but they had already told us they were flying out in two days. We only had until then to get Ben out of there.

We started coming up with a plan. We had yet to find Ben's insurance policy number. We didn't even know if he'd brought it with him, or had ever written it down. We sat up for a while, not really talking, just going over the same things, while I chain-smoked. We spoke to Mum, Naomi and Ben's great friend Miles, who had gone to the house to help out. We told them Ben was in a bad way but we mentioned nothing about the hospital. I don't think we said how bad Ben really was. They were worried enough; they didn't need any more reasons. We called it a night and attempted to sleep. Not much sleep came: only an hour or two. We woke up at 5.30am.

We called so many people the next day, I can't even remember who: the embassy, the hospital, various private hospitals. We'd found out that the hotel was owned by the Belgian ambassador and he was on his way to help. We also spoke to a guy my Uncle Oliver knew, and he came to the hotel too. I was amazed at how many people were trying to help. Neither Dad nor I spoke Spanish and we only had a phrase book, which wasn't exactly rammed with medical terms.

We got to the hospital and spotted Claudio, the man who had helped us find Ben the day before. You couldn't really miss him – the one calm presence amid the chaos. He told us to go and sit down and he would see if he could get us in again. The security at the hospital was as tight as an embassy's; there was another nasty-looking armed guard on the door. Claudio was successful, however, and again he told us to wait outside Ben's ward until someone came to get us.

We were waiting outside the ward for a long time. Some Dominican people were waiting, too, and trying to talk to us, to find out why we were there. We tried to explain and I think they got the gist because they stopped talking to us. We waited longer and longer. The heat and the smell in the place were rancid. All the time that we were waiting, trolleys were coming past us. People were bleeding, oozing, dying on only these bare metal trolleys. Then empty ones would come back, caked in old blood, smeared with fresh blood. No one seemed to give a fuck.

It must have been a good few hours before the door to the ward opened. There was a commotion. A trolley was wheeled out with a dead guy lying on it, face covered. My first thought was that it was Ben. It wasn't. I then wondered if it was the guy with the tube. We were allowed in now, and again we squeezed past the beds to get to Ben. There was just an empty, blood-stained bed where the guy with the bucket had been yesterday. I'm guessing he didn't make it through the night. I looked at all the guys as we walked past, and only recognised about one in eight. When we got to Ben, Dad did the same as he had the day before. Speaking to Ben, he touched his forehead, mopped his brow. He did his best to let him know we were there and tried to make him more comfortable.

We were by Ben's bedside for a while, until a doctor arrived with his entourage and asked us to follow him to his office. We were led through a rat run of corridors, past more rooms of the sick and injured, where the stench of rotting flesh was unbearable. There were flies everywhere and people sitting, lining the corridors, some on chairs, some on the floor, some with stab wounds, some with gunshot wounds, just sitting there, bleeding to death. I'm sure some of them were already dead. This was clearly normal, as the doctor just carried on walking to his office.

We finally got there: a room with no windows, shared with four or five other doctors and with only one desk. He explained the situation and it didn't sound good. They didn't have the medicine to treat Ben and they told us we would have to buy it ourselves from a shop down the road. We said we wanted to get Ben moved to a private hospital but the doctor said it was too dangerous to move him and they could do just as good a job there as anywhere else. I think his pride was hurt. I couldn't give a fuck! I wasn't going to let my brother lie there and die because some doctor thinks his hospital is as good as the next. We talked for a while longer, then left and bought everything on the doctor's list of medicines, dropping them back off at the ward. We were asked to leave again, so we headed back to the hotel.

When we got back, we tried again to find Ben's insurance details. I eventually found the policy number in a little black book, scribbled down on an empty page in the middle. Dad called home and passed it on. Miles had already been on the phone to various insurance companies, trying to find the one Ben had signed up with. Now he had it and the ball was rolling.

The man who owned the hotel arrived and came up with a list of private hospitals we could call and perhaps visit. We went to look at one but it didn't have an intensive care unit or people who specialised in brain injuries. Meanwhile, the phone kept ringing; all these different people – the insurance company and their medical experts – all trying to find the best place for Ben. The insurance company told us to leave it to them – they would find a place as soon as possible.

By this time, it was starting to get dark, so we headed back to see Ben. When we got to the hospital, Claudio wasn't hanging around the front as he usually was. We called him on his mobile, but no answer. We thought, *Fuck, we aren't going to get in.* Luckily, the hard-looking armed guard recognised us and let us pass. We walked up to the ward, where again we played the waiting game.

About ten yards down the corridor from us were two armed guards I hadn't seen before. They were having a heated discussion that soon turned into an argument. Dad and I were the only other people around, and tried not to watch. The argument escalated: these guys were really pissed off with each other. I'll never know why. Next thing we know, one of them pulls his gun and points it at the other, screaming and shouting. I'm standing there thinking, *Fuck, these guys are about to kill each other in a gun battle in the hospital! What the fuck is going on in this place?* We were only yards away. Luckily, the guy with the gun saw sense and lowered his weapon. At that moment the door to the ward was unlocked and we rushed in.

Ben was looking better; he didn't have such a high fever. The staff had been giving Ben the drugs we'd got him and they were clearly working. We were standing there, talking to Ben, trying to comfort him, when a policeman appeared. He had a clipboard, a photocopy of Ben's passport and of Jazz's. He had come to check Ben was still there, probably to see if he was still alive. He didn't speak English but the deputy he was with spoke a little and knew some French. He told us they'd arrested two guys. When we asked about Jazz, the policeman just shook his head. We tried to get more out of him but we were all finding the language barrier too much of a challenge. He gave us his card and left.

We left shortly after and Moreno drove us back to the hotel. There we spent more hours on the phone. Finally, we had a breakthrough. We found a private hospital that could take Ben and we managed to arrange for him to be moved the following morning. The insurance company agreed an ambulance crew could come to transfer him. We called Lourdes to explain the situation and she said she'd come and help as no doubt there'd be paperwork. We told the people in the hotel the good news. We both felt so relieved and happy. Ben would finally be in a proper hospital, with everything he needed.

Also, Mum and Naomi were arriving the next day, and they would never have to step inside the first hospital and have the same dreadful experience as we had. We were exhausted, but we both went to bed feeling that a massive weight had been lifted. I know I slept more than a few hours that night, and I'm guessing Dad did too, because he woke me up with his snoring.

We woke early again. Today was the day. Ben was being moved. We spoke to Lourdes. She said she would get to Dario Contreras hospital as soon as she could but that she had things to do first. We knew this meant we couldn't count on her help. We'd become quite friendly with a Haitian called Paul, who worked at the hotel. He spoke French, Spanish and a tiny bit of English and he very kindly offered to come with us to help out. We got to the hospital, found Claudio and went in – no problem. He took us to the chairs we'd been sitting on that first night.

On the same floor that Ben's ward was on, in the doctor's common room, which also served as an office, the phone rang. It was the insurance company: the ambulance was on its way. We waited about an hour before the ambulance crew turned up: two guys in uniform, looking very smart, clean and professional. They seemed to know what they were doing. They went onto the ward to get Ben ready. We waited some more, then the doctor who was caring for Ben came rushing around the corner with his entourage, looking pissed off. He told us we couldn't move Ben – it was too dangerous. Dad was trying to explain that it was what the insurance company's medical team had suggested, but the doctor wasn't happy. He kept trying to convince us otherwise. I lost my temper with him and told him in no uncertain terms that there was no way I'd be letting my brother stay there, or he would die. I felt like saying, *This isn't about your pride as a doctor. This is about my brother staying alive.* He made Dad sign a piece of paper saying we were moving him against all medical advice and, because they weren't clear about where to sign the document because of the language barrier, Dad had to leave ink fingerprints in various places all over it. The doctor wished us luck and walked off.

We were left waiting on those seats for ages. One of the ambulance guys came up and said there was a problem. My heart sank. I immediately thought he was going to tell us Ben had died. He hadn't, but when they had taken him off the ventilator both his lungs had collapsed. They'd managed to inflate them again when they connected him to the ambulance's portable ventilator. Now they were just waiting to see if it was safe to move him. They were pretty unsure about this because the doctor was obviously in there trying to persuade them against it.

After another half-an-hour or so, the ambulance trolley came around the corner carrying Ben. The trolley was spotless, not like the metal ones in the hospital, caked in blood. They were just about to wheel Ben into the lift when the phone rang again. It was the insurance company; the plan had changed and Ben would now be taken to a private clinic, Clínica Corazones Unidos, not to the private hospital we had identified earlier. The consultant doctor in Miami who was advising the insurance company convinced us it was the best place in Santo Domingo for Ben, and we only found out later that he had had to argue with the insurance company until they agreed he could go there.

The ambulance was waiting when we came out of the hospital. We said goodbye to Claudio and thanked him for his help. Ben was loaded into the ambulance and Dad got in the back with him. I walked round to the front, past the nasty-looking security guard, who smiled at me and gave me a pat on the back. I got a sense he was relieved for us – he knew we were off to somewhere good. I jumped in the front and the sirens went on. We were off.

The drive that followed was the most terrifying experience of my life. The guy at the wheel was driving like a nutter, speeding down the road, squeezing through the tightest gaps between cars, lorries and mopeds. I honestly thought we were going to crash. To be fair to him, he was actually an excellent driver, but it didn't make the journey any less nerve-wracking. One gap really was too tight. He shot between two lorries, swerved through a gap to the left, then across through another gap to the right, two lanes over, all at about 60 miles an hour. We got so close to a guy on his moped that he swerved up onto the pavement and went flying off his bike. It happened so quickly I don't think the driver realised – or he just didn't care. We must have got to the clinic in record time.

We pulled up outside the clinic. A crew of medics, both doctors and nurses, was waiting for us. They surrounded Ben as he was wheeled away from the ambulance and rushed him into a room. Dad and I were left in the lobby. It was bright, super-clean and air-conditioned, with a marble floor. The place was sparkling compared to where we had been. We got the sense we were in the right place and in safe hands. The doctor came to see us. He explained they needed to assess Ben, wash him and start looking after him, and said we should come back later.

We headed back to the hotel, incredibly relieved and happy. We had done what we'd set out to do. We had moved Ben out of that hell-hole and into a decent hospital. He was safe now and he would get the best care available. I was over the moon. On top of that, Mum and Naomi's plane was landing in only a few hours – but we had cut it very fine.

Jenny, Ben's mum

That late-night knock on the door – every parent's worst nightmare – propelled us into events, emotions and a whole new world that would change us all forever. Those first days of separation from Hugh and Theo were so hard. Fearing the worst while anxiously waiting for news, always wondering but not being able to really imagine what Hugh and Theo were facing, meant Naomi and I lived in a kind of virtual reality. The time difference didn't help.

We were kept busy trying to find anything at home relating to Ben's insurance, and relied on Ben's friends to pass the bad news among themselves. When your children have left home and you need to seek critical information, such as email passwords, you realise how little you really know about their lives, their work and their colleagues. But word spread quickly via social media; it was amazing how fast people heard and got in touch. Friends of ours and Ben's set up communication hubs to save us being at the end of constant enquiries and having to spend our fractured energy repeating the awful news without much new to add.

Then, not 12 hours since the knock on the door, I was listening to Jazz's mother, Abby, over the phone, her voice full of raw sorrow yet so generous in her willingness to support us with all her good wishes. Two mothers linked by a tragedy: one who'd lost everything, the other clinging to hope. Abby was always generous with her own optimism about Ben, always keen for me to know that a good outcome was what Jazz would have wanted.

Naomi and I made the journey to the Dominican Republic 48

hours after Hugh's and Theo's departure, carrying our heavy burden of uncertainty, the two of us sleep-deprived, only adrenaline keeping us going as we merged with the throng of travellers making their way through the departure lounge of our local UK airport. We waited for our flight supported by regular text messages sending us love and kindness, connecting us with all we had left behind.

In the arrivals lounge of Santo Domingo's airport, the heat carried the unique smell of somewhere tropical and exotic. Surrounded by a babble of Spanish that we couldn't understand, we felt alien and lost. Then there they were: Hugh and Theo. What a relief to be all together.

I remember asking Hugh, even before we left the airport, whether Ben had facial injuries. No – some stitches and an awful black eye. At least, I thought with some small comfort, if he lives, he'll still have his face – his beautiful blue eyes and the features that make up who he is. One thing less for him to cope with, whatever else the future holds.

That evening, Moreno drove us to the clinic, where the consultant in charge of Ben's care, Dr Valenzuela, was waiting to brief us. This special man was so professional, and always frank and brutally honest – yet he also had bucketfuls of humanity, for which I will always be grateful. He was a skilled communicator, with a readiness to answer our questions and queries. As the days progressed we got the hang of getting the most out of our brief daily meetings with him.

He allowed each of us to spend ten minutes with Ben, three times a day: late morning, late afternoon and evening. On our first meeting he explicitly described what he expected from us – no drama, no tears, a brightness in our voices when we spoke to Ben. We had to communicate as normally as possible. And then he suggested we pray. We are not a family with any particular faith and this must have shown in our faces, because he continued by saying, 'Well, draw on whatever gives you strength.'

That first day, after giving us his instructions, the consultant told us we should now go and see Ben, one at a time. My heart thumped: should I go first, if the others didn't want to? I can't even remember the order we took that first time. However, I do remember the instructions anchored me: the brightness of voice, the need to talk about ordinary things and things that would usually interest Ben. Leaving the others on the brown foyer sofas, and not knowing what I would see or how I would cope with it, I slipped through the door of Ben's intensive care ward, put on a gown, pumped the anti-bacterial gel, and turned to see Ben – recognisably Ben – at the other end of the room.

I walked past the nurses at the desk to the side of his high bed. He was connected to so many tubes – in his hands, arms and neck – and he had a mask to help him breathe. There were all sorts of blinking, whirring, beeping machines producing readings I didn't dare look at too closely – strange noises and a multitude of wavy lines: an indication of his life supported.

Ben was lying quite still, but once in a while his arms would extend with his wrists turned inwards, fists clenched. Initially I thought these stretch-like movements showed some positive sign, only for the consultant to explain that they were a primitive movement known as extensor reflexes and were, rather, a grim indication of the nature and extent of the trauma: with parts of the brain disconnected from each other, only the primitive brain is evident. Thus the frequency of these reflexes was something the three of us discussed and reported back to Dr Valenzuela, and during our stay in the Dominican Republic we agreed that these were becoming less pronounced as well as less frequent.

Dr Valenzuela, lead consultant at Clínica Corazones Unidos

My ten minutes always took on the same pattern. I guess it helped me to keep going, to let him know it was me, and provided a structure that fitted into the time slot.

I gave my usual greeting, the one I normally gave in response to his arriving home on a fleeting visit or to an impromptu phone conversation. I hope my tone expressed a mother's delight at an unexpected snatch of time with a child who had left home long ago. I always greeted him using his name or the family nickname and I always said it was me, Mum. Then I made mundane comments about the day: about the downpours and the noise of the rain clattering on the skylight above his bed; about the familiar characters we'd passed on the way and if anything unusual had happened to them; who we'd had messages from with news of home; who had sent him positive vibes; and who sent their love – here, a light touch on his arm where a space between the tubes allowed. As I talked, against the increasingly familiar background noise of the medical equipment, the bleeps and lines on the monitor changed rhythms. One, in particular, always went up. All three of us commented on this and took it as an indication that Ben was tuning in at some level and our time with him had some purposeful effect.

There were always two nurses assigned to the intensive care unit and, since Ben was mostly on his own, all their attention went to him. Sometimes I'd walk in to shrieks of laughter and animated chatter, to find two or sometimes three staff piled onto the bed next to Ben, sharing a joke or just being near him and not at their desk. I liked the fact there was laughter and jollity around him, especially as in our own time with him, each one of us alone, we would have found it nigh on impossible to have a rip-roaring, one-way laugh.

While we never really shared the details of our individual times with Ben, I know we each spent our allotted ten minutes differently. Naomi read to him. She found that easiest. She told us that sometimes one of the medical orderlies would come and stand next to her if he was on the ward, which unnerved her. I'm sure he was simply trying to fathom why she was reading out some vampire story. Hugh often did the crossword, thinking aloud, asking Ben for help with clues. Theo says he talked a stream of rubbish – 'just a load of shit' was how he put it. We all shared how we got better at filling the minutes with our own monologues, sometimes accidentally going over our allotted time.

After a couple of days, the consultant suggested Ben heard some music and messages from friends. Naomi and Theo put out the call and an eclectic mix of contributions swiftly came back. They compiled a selection, some items longer than others, all interesting, all with the easy language and banter adopted by good friends. So, after our morning or afternoon visit, Theo would often set the iPod going, fit the ear pieces on Ben (having checked the volume) and leave him with the latest compilation.

As we each became more confident with our visiting routines, we asked Dr Valenzuela why we couldn't visit together. He was very clear that we would be talking among ourselves and lose the focus on Ben. Our chatter would become background noise with little meaning to Ben and likely to cause unwelcomed stress. Establishing a calm routine with clearly identifiable sounds such as our voices or music was seen as reducing anxiety, a state often recognised in patients with injuries such as Ben's. When we got back to the UK we kept similar routines for our visits to the ICU (intensive care unit) visits, even as Ben slowly became more responsive.

Having spent one night, all four of us together, in what we called 'Jazz and Ben's hotel', we moved to be within walking distance of Ben. The staff on the reception desk at our new hotel soon knew our circumstances and began to ask how our visits had been and what news there was. They saw us leave, regular as clockwork, three times a day, to make the 15-minute walk to the clinic. With the heat, the humidity, the sudden downpours and having to run the gauntlet of road networks not built with pedestrians in mind, we four 'foreigners' must have made a sight as we uncertainly traversed town. We'd all developed a lack of confidence in crossing the road, and only did so when we were totally happy that the distance between cars allowed us to cross with the greatest possible safety margin.

Our route took us the same way each day, passing the money lender, legless in his wheelchair; the fruit seller in the residential area; the Austrian coffee shop; and the final landmark – the fantastic screw pine, often offset by a deep blue sky, which signalled we were nearly at the clinic. We also passed an imposing church, which at first we hadn't acknowledged as one of our landmarks, but which became so in time.

The first week saw many ups and downs, dips and turns, as Ben pulled through and rallied, only to relapse – yet all the time he tenaciously clung to life. Within a couple of days his scans showed the swelling of his brain had reduced significantly. We crowded around the illuminated screen in the ICU to be given an idiot's guide to brain anatomy. The original brainstem bleed, the cause of much pessimism, was now difficult to see on the scan. On day five he had a chest infection, and in their usual frank style the doctors told us this was often fatal in cases such as Ben's. But Ben responded to his mix of antibiotics and fought the infection off. The deep grazes and abrasions across his chest, hand and feet were not healing well but an infection here, too, was quickly identified, and once new dressings were applied with the right antibiotic, it wasn't long before the doctor in charge of infectious diseases was satisfied they'd cracked it.

We became regulars in the hospital foyer, waiting for our twice-daily updates and individual turns to visit Ben. There were other families there, too, and one in particular would greet us each morning and kiss us goodnight if we were still there late, as they often were as they awaited news of their sick grandma, who was Ben's only companion in the ICU. Their warmth and compassion touched us. They'd ask after Ben even though our answers were always much the same. They were always enquiring but never invasive. It wasn't long before they told us he was part of their daily prayers. I hope my response was sufficiently grateful and unmarked by my own lack of faith. Later, they announced Ben was now part of their church's regular prayers. With great cheerfulness they told us the congregation were all rooting for him. It turned out their church was the great big one we passed every day in our comings and goings, and we thanked them for their positive vibes.

During our second week in this routine, we were approaching the clinic when members of this family rushed out to greet us with great excitement, telling us to hurry, as Ben had opened his eyes – a sign their prayers had been heard. They'd witnessed this while visiting their grandma.

The excitement of Ben's 'awakening' sent us running into the foyer. He had opened his eyes – but we'd missed it, and he didn't do so again that day. In fact, whether Ben opened his eyes became a bit of a yardstick for our visits and it was the key thing we'd always report to each other after going in to see him. However, if we were lucky enough to be there when he did open his eyes, his stare was constant and unresponsive both to sound and movement. So it was a first step, but still with so many unknowns.

Dr Valenzuela explained all the issues and shared his concerns, such as the danger of infection or the implications of Ben's primitive arm reflexes, always framing them within the contexts of what was critical and which concerns had immediate or long-term impact. We were always told when the dangers had passed.

After day six or seven, the feedback sessions took on a slightly more hopeful tone. Dr Valenzuela felt able to share his views on Ben's progress over these early days, which he put down to three key elements. Firstly, he talked about the 'golden' minutes and the first 24 hours. The response of those nearby doctors in the first minutes, and the speed with which Ben arrived at hospital after the accident, had been incredibly fortuitous. Then Ben's age, though not that young at 27, was still considered the right end of the youth continuum. Lastly, there was his excellent level of fitness. The consultant commented that Ben had excellent lungs and couldn't believe it when we told him Ben was a smoker. He shared these views with some small measure of optimism, particularly when Ben rallied after each setback, such as his high fever, lung infection and infected skin on his chest and hands.

Dr Valenzuela's other key message, which stayed with us over the weeks and months to come, was to always follow the patient. He told us the long road ahead for all of us could not be dictated by our own agendas; Ben would be the one to set the pace, the speed of progress, and by following the patient we would be in tune with what we could expect of him. That was the best advice and became a bit of a mantra we all trotted out when Ben surprised us or took a direction we weren't prepared for.

The doctor was keen for us to get home. He felt Ben would get better care in the UK and that, as a family, we needed to be close to relatives and friends, with all the support that would bring. He also said he thought Ben would make significant progress. He never defined this for us, except to say the first year would see the greatest progress and the second less so. He left us with no illusions; what we faced was still uncertain. Nonetheless, he had given us a most encouraging prognosis. We left feeling optimistic that Ben would not remain in a vegetative state and we wouldn't one day have to face the terrible decision of whether to turn off his life support. As we concluded our last family feedback session with him, I realised it was the first time I'd thanked someone and truly felt that words couldn't express my gratitude.

Once Ben had been confirmed safe to move by air ambulance, we waited for the insurance company to locate an aircraft with all the medical equipment needed to provide intensive care, and to put together the right team of specialist nurses and doctors and to care for Ben on his journey home.

Once again we were to be separated. Hugh was to travel back with Ben and the rest of us would fly on ahead to confirm the final arrangements for Ben's transfer to our nearest ICU. We would all be back together a few days later at a local hospital, full of hope and expectation about the level of medical care and attention Ben would receive in the UK.

Naomi, Ben's sister

Saturday, 18 September 2010. I'd been out with friends the night before and woke with a start at 7am. I didn't know why. I felt upset but I had no reason to feel that way. I decided to jump on a train down to Brighton. This might not seem that unusual, but at the time it was quite out of character – to be upset and teary, for one thing; and secondly to jump on a train to go and see my mum and dad without planning it weeks in advance.

When I saw Dad in the driveway as I arrived home, I instantly burst into tears. The first thing he asked was whether there was a problem with my health (I'd been treated for thyroid cancer two years before). I reassured him it wasn't but I still couldn't explain. I then did the same when I saw Mum. I didn't know what was wrong, but I felt convinced that something was.

That night, I found out about Ben, and it emerged that he and Jazz had been hit by the car around the time I'd woken up feeling strange. I've never experienced anything like that before or since. Perhaps it was a weird coincidence, perhaps not, but somehow when I woke I knew something was wrong.

When I heard the hammering on my parents' front door in the middle of the night, my first thoughts were that Theo had forgotten his keys. *But why would he bang so hard, and why wouldn't he just have phoned me?* I thought it might be some drunk person. I didn't want to open it, so I stood behind Dad. The next few minutes felt like some movie scene: *Can we come in? Are you Benjamin Clench's father? I think you should sit down. Benjamin is in a coma. The person he was with has been killed.*

At that point I ran upstairs to my parents' bedroom – I had to wake Mum. I remember feeling as though I couldn't breathe, and Mum being so calm. She told me of course Ben wouldn't die. I remember feeling helpless, distraught; what would I do, what would we all do, if he died?

Ben and I had become very close in the few years before his accident. He'd been
living on a barge and spent a winter on the canal around the cor-

ner from where I lived in London. We socialised with each other's friends and had enjoyed a particularly fun and drunken summer in the weeks before his accident.

Naomi, Ben and Theo in Paris, September 2010, the week before the accident

When I returned to my flat in London after being diagnosed with thyroid cancer, Ben came over and made me eggs Florentine, and hugged me quietly on the sofa while I had a silent weep. He once picked me up after one of my operations while suffering a killer hangover. Being a nervous new driver, he drove me home jerking the car all the way. It was incredibly painful, but we laughed about it eventually. While late-night boozing after a night out, Ben often tried to persuade me that my current squeeze was a dickhead, but he also called me for advice when things had been tricky with Jazz, or at three in the morning when he'd locked himself out.

So, as far as brother-sister relationships go, I'd say we were pretty close. But this was a recent thing – it wasn't until I was 18 that Ben told me he'd forgiven me for being mean to him when I was little. I can't remember any of it, but supposedly he adored me and I was pretty harsh with him.

After the police visit, the next few hours and days were purely functional; calmly phoning people to let them know. However, there was a disconnect between some of the more functional aspects to my day, and being scared of the cars outside when we left the house to get some fresh air. Being amazed the world still went on. I found it astounding people could just walk around like nothing had happened when our world was seemingly falling apart.

Travelling to the Dominican Republic a few days later, it suddenly struck me that not everyone on an aeroplane is off on a happy holiday. In fact, you might be getting on a plane to live out your worst nightmare. Suddenly, life seemed more fragile than ever before. Everyday tasks were difficult – arranging travel insurance or calling the bank to let them know we would be abroad. Every time the phone rang, I'd listen at the top of the stairs to see it if was Dad or Theo letting us know Ben had died. Mum and I shared a bed for those first few days.

The kindness of friends and family was heartfelt and touching. I learned from this experience that if someone you know is going through something horrific, just letting them know you're thinking of them is all that's needed.

Mum was so incredibly calm through everything. I don't know if it was a mother's instinct that Ben would be okay, or to protect her family, but I'm not sure I ever saw my mum cry. Dad, on the other hand, was struggling to keep it together. Skyping Dad and Theo shortly after they'd seen Ben, I remember feeling so grateful Theo had drunkenly demanded he go too. He was clearly holding Dad up. Theo sat with his arm around Dad as he wept and told me life was never going to be the same. Dad managed to convey how bad things were, and if Ben survived, he was going to be a vegetable or unable to function on any level.

The first time I saw Ben in the Dominican Republic, he was in the private clinic, which thankfully was calm and clean. I wasn't the first to go in – I was too nervous. My heart was in my throat, not knowing what to expect. We'd been told not to let on we were upset – always talk to Ben with a smile, the doctor said. So that's what I did, through tears. He looked so vulnerable and helpless. He'd been cleaned up and, considering the state we knew he was in, looked relatively intact physically, apart from some nasty grazing and a black eye.

That first night, we stayed in the hotel Ben and Jazz had been in. We were all staying in one room with two double beds. Theo let go that night – he absolutely sobbed in bed next to me and told me it wasn't going to be okay.

Our time in the Dominican Republic was filled with a routine: visiting Ben at our allocated visiting hours; picking up messages from his friends back home to play to him on repeat; making playlists of his favourite songs. I would read to him every visit. It helped to keep me focused and also gave me something to say, as his accident was the only thing in our lives at that time. I'd bought the vampire romance *Twilight* at the airport and I knew Ben would be horrified I was reading him such a crappy book – I took some comfort in knowing he'd see the funny side when he woke up.

It's funny what you find comfort in and what is all too much. I hated the heat, the traffic and that the locals walked around so slowly, like the world was never going to end. But I felt soothed by the emails and messages from home. I also remember the day a lady at the hospital whose mother had been in intensive care came and gave me a small image of the Virgin Mary. She told me her whole congregation had been saying a prayer for Ben. For the first time ever, I understood how people can find solace in religion.

Ben

I have since listened to the music and friends' messages that were played to me on an iPod when I was still in a coma, and it was good to hear it all again. It offers a snapshot of how everyone was dealing with that terrible news, and listening to it makes me reflect on a time when my mind was having to deal with the trauma forced upon me. I hope I found the music soothing. However, the singing by a group of my friends was utterly horrendous – certainly a good effort to wake me up.

I can immediately recognise all the music my friends and siblings chose. I can imagine some of them selecting certain tracks as safe options, with upbeat and cheerful sounds, but there are some quite raucous 'Wake up, Ben!' inclusions, too. Hearing the messages from my friends and family is touching, as I can understand how difficult it was for people to record them. I realise it would have been an incredibly tough thing to do – when you want to sound optimistic, yet there is very little to be optimistic about. It reminds me how lucky I am to have so many friends and family in my life who were rooting for me to pull through.

Hugh

On Tuesday, 5 October, just two-and-a-half weeks after the accident, the insurance company arranged for Ben to be repatriated in a private jet kitted out as an ambulance, accompanied by a doctor and two specialist nurses from Toronto. The plane arrived in the Dominican Republic from Canada, and it was agreed I would accompany Ben on the flight. As before, he was prepared for the transfer while the medics conferred about his care and the drug regime he was on. The aeroplane team left the hospital armed with a large holdall full of various drugs.

I asked the ambulance driver to go carefully, as there was no need to rush and throw Ben around like last time. We drove through a security gate and directly onto the tarmac in the oppressive heat of early evening. The Canadian medical staff were in green-badged boiler suits and looked every inch the part. The nurses, in particular, looked like Wonder Woman clones. They talked in jargon and exuded professionalism.

Our flight was long and cramped, with just enough space for me to crouch in the back of the fuselage. One of the nurses attended to Ben the whole time, ensuring he was receiving enough oxygen. We touched down in Montréal to refuel and, as soon as the plane came to a halt, vehicles drove up with fresh supplies for us and to refuel the plane. We then touched down in Labrador at an army airfield, where we left the plane for half-an-hour to use the toilet (there wasn't one on the plane) and to have a cup of coffee alongside various military personnel. We also had a connecting flight in Iceland where, as the plane door opened, a freezing blast of air startled Ben and he opened his eyes and looked around. I was greatly encouraged by this, as I was by the knowledge that we were nearly home, where all would be well and the nightmare over.

Ben

I was extremely lucky to get into such a good hospital in the Dominican Republic, thanks to having health insurance. It gives me renewed faith in health insurance companies. In my case, for a mere ten-pound premium, the company spent close to ninety-thousand pounds on my medical care and repatriation by air ambulance. It's hard to imagine how the companies can survive when they offer such benefits. I suppose it shows how unusual cases like mine are, if all the other

Last stop, in Iceland, in the air ambulance that flew Ben and me back to the UK in October 2010

ten-pound premiums that are never claimed against can fund such expensive care and still leave money to keep the company in profit.

Of course, it was also fortunate Mum and Dad nagged me so much about getting travel insurance in the first place. I almost didn't get any because I couldn't find a policy that would cover me for kidnap, which I had become especially worried about. In the end, I'd quickly bought some cheap health insurance on their insistence.

The repatriation flight sounds quite impressive and dramatic. It's a shame I wasn't awake to appreciate it all. However, my memory of going to the Dominican Republic in the first place is all gone. It's somewhere I would like to revisit, to see if anything comes back by being there.

*

The air ambulance medics, Shim, Diane, and Christine

Hearing Ben had landed safely back in the UK (albeit still unconscious) felt like a massive achievement that made me want to celebrate, despite all the other conflicting emotions.

Robbie Barkell, a friend of Ben's and Jazz's from the London School of Economics

*

Hugh

Our final landing was at Gatwick Airport, where we were met on the tarmac by another private ambulance. Unfortunately, the ventilator equipment in this one was faulty – the first such failure we'd encountered – and Ben had to be manually ventilated as the driver's sat-nav led us by the shortest but almost unnavigable route through country lanes to the hospital that would care for Ben.

I'd rung the hospital on landing to let them know we'd be there shortly and Jenny had also rung ahead to warn them. I was greatly relieved to reach what I thought would be Ben's salvation but, as we arrived at A&E (Accident & Emergency) looking like something from a Superman film, with the medics in their smart blue uniforms, we were greeted with, 'Who are you?' The reception desk had no idea we were coming.

This was the beginning of our complete disillusionment with the National Health Service (NHS). While we were in the Dominican Republic we had access to Ben's consultant at least twice a day. As well as updating us on Ben's condition and treatment, he was very good at reassuring us generally. To this day we still don't know who had responsibility for Ben once he entered the intensive care unit in the UK hospital. It was always a battle to see any doctor to update us, and the doctor on duty seemed to be different every time we visited.

We'd brought with us a veritable medicine chest of drugs, several of which were antibiotics prescribed for Ben because the tubes feeding him air generally cause lung infections that can be very dangerous and even fatal. However, the first doctor we managed to see told us it was not NHS policy to administer antibiotic 'cocktails' and immediately ceased them, despite the fact they'd been carefully selected based on an analysis of Ben's existing infections. It had been a continual battle to keep these at bay and, within two days of the withdrawal of these drugs, Ben suffered a collapsed lung. In the Dominican Republic the clinic would carry out an immediate assessment of the bacteria infecting him. The results would return on the same day and his drug regime adjusted accordingly. In the UK it could take three or even four days to get a result if the sample was taken just before the weekend.

The UK doctors were dismissive of the standards of health care in the Dominican Republic and placed Ben in an isolation ward on the assumption he would be carrying multiple infections. Our first-hand experience was the complete reverse, with Third World standards prevailing in the UK, where Ben soon contracted MRSA (Methicillin-Resistant Staphylococcus Aureus).

I visited him three times a day for several months, and during his time in the intensive care unit it was rare to see the same nurse in charge of his care. On one occasion it was apparent to me he was in distress, as he kept pulling at his catheter. I suggested to the nurse it might be blocked and needed to be dealt with. I later learned it was not until seven hours later, at 11pm, that a new nurse identified the problem himself and dealt with it. He told me he'd collected 1.5 litres of urine from Ben. A normal full bladder contains about 400 millilitres.

We completely lost faith in the standards of care in the ICU. I felt compelled to ring each night immediately before going to bed to check Ben was settled and not in distress. I raised the issue of continuity of care with the ICU staff, who told me careful records are kept of each patient and they regarded this as sufficient in handing over to a new nurse. This was in no way borne out by our experience, and it transpired the nurses there worked three long shifts per week of 12-13 hours, followed by four days off. This employment pattern was the reason for the frequent changes of nursing care and, while it may suit an employee to have four days free per week, it did not appear to us to be in the best interests of patient care. During the three weeks Ben was in the ICU he had the same nurse he had had before on only a handful of occasions.

We later experienced a very similar pattern in the neuro-rehabilitation unit, which was a dark and depressing ward on the lower ground floor of this apparently modern hospital. Many of the nursing staff were supplied by agencies, and the regular staff seemed continually stressed and undermanned. On one occasion during Ben's three-month stay in the hospital, we were phoned at home on a Saturday and asked to come in that day as there were insufficient staff on duty to meet the needs of all the patients, the majority of whom were stroke victims.

Ben had had a tracheotomy soon after arriving at the hospital. This is a hole made directly into the trachea through the throat so a breathing tube can be inserted for those who cannot breathe independently, and is more comfortable for the patient than a breathing tube inserted through the mouth. When the breathing tube was eventually removed, a plaster was put over the hole while it healed. This dressing was never changed and after two weeks or so I asked if it ought to be. The nurse supposedly caring for Ben at the time did not feel confident enough to remove it, despite several requests. Consequently, I removed it myself, revealing a green and pussy goo that had accumulated over the fortnight. I still find it hard to believe an NHS hospital could be so negligent and unable to perform such basic tasks.

Among the things agency staff were required to do was to keep a record throughout the night of Ben's wakefulness. After some weeks we noticed he would often wake in the night and be unable to get back to sleep, although he did manage to do so after using the toilet. At the time, Ben was unable express his needs, let alone find his way to the toilet, even though it was *en suite*. Once we realised this, and even though it was recorded in his notes, we pinned a large sign up in his room to tell the nurse to take him to the toilet if he woke in the night, because we had long stopped trusting the staff to act on the instructions in Ben's file. During his stay in the neuro-rehabilitation unit, Ben would only be bathed if we specifically requested it.

We were by no means alone in the difficulties we experienced with the nursing care in this unit. The elderly husband of a stroke victim was very distressed at the standard of care his wife was receiving. The family of another young man who'd suffered a severe head injury made a formal complaint, which we contributed to. While this was dealt with sensitively and carefully by one of the managers, we didn't see any impact on the day-to-day running of the unit.

Before Ben's accident we would have defended the NHS to the hilt, but our experience with Ben has been so poor we can no longer do so. While there are many admirable and excellent individuals within the NHS, there is a lack of personal responsibility incorporated into the management structure. Where staff do take personal responsibility, it is entirely through their own volition. Most simply walk away at the end of their shift, job done or not.

Ben

Imagine waking up in a place you don't know, where you don't know who you are or why you are there; opening your eyes and being enveloped in the almighty confusion of not knowing anything at all. This isn't the same as simply not remembering or understanding your situation. It is an all-encompassing mystery and hits you hard at every level of your being. Your sense of self is completely dissolved. This was exactly my situation in October 2010.

Being struck with this level of amnesia is totally engrossing and utterly scary to live with, although at the same time it is all you know and you can't compare it to not having amnesia because you've forgotten what it's like not to have it. Your whole life has been ripped away from you.

My experience of coming out of the coma was slow and confused. There was no dramatic 'waking up' moment, just a gradual dawning of understanding – or, to be honest, a lack of understanding. To start with, the constant uncertainty is something that hangs over your every move. It coils and wraps around you, and can't be disentangled. My confusion was intense.

So much of your very being has been taken from you that there is no memory to fall back on with any security. There is no recognition to be found anywhere. These people around you tell you they are your family, but you don't recognise them and the questions you ask can be very specific and sometimes profound. You are asking your parents things like, *How do I know you are my parents?*

Jenny

'Zero' is the period Ben spent on life-support: the rhythmic sound of the machine that pumped air in and out; the many drips and cannulas in his hands, arms and neck giving him the liquids and drugs that nourished him and kept infections at bay; the bleeping of machines and the lines on monitors that made sense only to the medical team. Zero was also a time of internal turmoil, anxiety and living in the moment, fearing the worst and hoping for the best. But the best is, at this stage, a life supported. For me it meant those violent swings from high anxiety, thumping heart, despair and hopelessness to wishing so desperately for something that I couldn't change or undo, ever. Zero was a time when our despair and desolation were reflected onto each other as we hit our highs and lows. Zero was also a time when the smallest change gave us disproportionate hope that Ben might, just might, pull through.

A slight shift from Zero is 'Eyes Wide Open', first witnessed and joyously conveyed to us by the lovely family at the clinic in the Dominican Republic. Eyes Wide Open but without focus, gaze or tracking in response to sound, movement or images. We longed for Eyes Wide Open during our visits, as this became the evidence of a huge step forward. But this exciting change was tempered by the consultant's response that, although this showed a level of awakening, it was only a normal stage following such trauma, and not a pre-determinant or even a prediction of progress or recovery. When Ben was transferred to the UK, this was how close to Zero he remained. Or how far from Zero he had travelled.

The period in intensive care back in the UK saw Ben start to focus more when his eyes were open. He began to track movement and turn towards sounds. He began to respond to individual voices. This made us bring things in to provide greater interest during our visits, with more opportunities to interact with Ben differently from how we had in the Dominican Republic.

A thoughtful nurse had asked if we could bring in photos of Ben so the staff could see him with his real identity, not defined by the machines and the procedures they performed for him. Before long, we began to share what we'd brought in for the staff with Ben. There were photographs of when he was on his narrowboat in London the year before, when he lived on the canals while doing his master's, and family photos of recent holidays which, in hindsight, were not the best choice as we later realised his long-term memory was far better; events that had taken place up to two or three years before meant nothing to him.

When he was better able to communicate with us, it was obvious how little he could connect with. As he made progress over the months, and for as long as the first couple of years after the accident, his memory 'holes' became a feature of who he was. His memory bank had so much missing.

Little by little, Ben went from being flat on his back to a slightly raised position. We would raise his bed's back support so he could better see the photographs we had brought to show him. In time, when we mentioned people by name, he started to seek out particular photographs on the large board we had fixed them onto. We also found that the notes his visitors had stuck to the wall gave us something to talk to him about and fuelled our one-sided conversation in a way that involved him, despite the fact he couldn't respond. Even without knowing how much he was taking in, this was now a long way from those first monological visits in the Dominican Republic.

Ben continued to leave Zero behind over the next few weeks. His progress began to take off in all sorts of different ways. There was an emergence of certain things he could have some control over, such as the beginnings of indicating yes or no by directing his gaze or following simple instructions. Other changes became quite dominant, such as his restless legs, over which he had no control. He soon became so restless that his bed was made up on the floor to stop him hurting himself if he fell out. We never knew how he managed to turn himself around 180 degrees, still attached to all his feeding tubes, but he would often be found facing the opposite direction. Sometimes he would get his legs stuck between the bars at the sides of the bed or knock his feet on these through violent and uncontrolled movements. The father of another young man with a serious head injury told me his son had also done this – he'd completely forgotten about it until I asked. It was reassuring to think of it as a stage that would pass. We all became adept at foot and leg massage and it seemed to calm him when he was particularly restless. After a while, the nurses commented that Ben's feet were in particularly good shape, with good tone and, of course, beautifully soft skin – so the massage did more than just soothe and distract him.

In the last couple of weeks in the ICU, before he was transferred to the neuro-rehabilitation ward, Ben began to sit in a wheelchair, with a strap around his chest to help his sitting position and stop him sliding off. His head, too heavy for his weakened muscles, often hung down and his inability to swallow resulted in dribble, which he couldn't control, but with each session he grew a little stronger. It was such a joy to see him out of bed, despite the effort it took him to sit. His weight-loss of 20kg seemed more noticeable in his chair. Away from the bed his frame was much diminished, his stick-like legs poking out of the regulation hospital gown.

In some of the visits from the physiotherapy team they placed Ben on a swivel board, which slowly rotated him upright and held him there for very short periods in that weightless but standing position. After that, he showed a desire to stand whenever we sat him on the edge of the bed. He seemed to want to get up and made a distinct effort to push his feet to the floor and lever himself down against our supporting arms, accompanied by whoops of surprise from us. His muscle memory had been awakened.

We all began to notice further signs of Ben's increasing awareness. There was a noticeable change in how he looked at us when we talked about things that interested him. The staff who nursed him most regularly were equally chuffed. They suggested we bring in his music or some DVDs, and he started to tap into these for increasing periods of time. He would watch the screen of the little DVD player, quite mesmerised and captivated. He now had recognisable 'yes' and 'no' signs, making it easy for us to know whether or not he wanted to listen to music or watch a DVD. How much he got out of these activities, I don't know, but this was the beginning of so many things we did with Ben to help him regain the skills he would need as part of the long road ahead.

These early stages shaped our behaviour with Ben. Hugh and I commented on how Ben's dependence, so reminiscent of infancy, brought out parental instincts we'd thought were long gone. We became protective and fiercely Ben-centric, trying to find a balance between being pushy parents and reasonable parents in an alien medical environment that didn't always welcome our questioning, our standards or our expectations in relation to Ben's treatment or therapies.

We generally limited visits to the ICU to immediate and close family. I guess this was partly because we didn't want to overcrowd Ben and wanted the focus to stay one-to-one. Hugh visited three times a day, every day, unless this meant Ben would be over-visited, and the rest of us would fit around this schedule. This worked well, allowing each of us to fulfil our need to spend time with Ben but also to do what we had to do away from the hospital. Also, we also didn't want Ben's friends to see him at this stage – we thought they might be distressed, which would then upset Ben and the rest of us.

However, we broke this rule for Miles, his close university friend and flatmate over many years, who visited regularly and often came with Naomi, sharing the journey from London over the many weeks to come. Ben's siblings remained committed to regular visits, though squeezing these in after work meant long days. Ben's friends supported Naomi, who lived and worked in London, looking out for her, inviting her round for a meal or sharing the journey with her once he was transferred to the rehab ward and visiting became more open to friends. All our networks remained true and constant in their support, buoying us up.

The defining element that would allow Ben to transfer to the rehab ward was for his breathing to be independent of any support and free of his tracheotomy. This was achieved under careful control. Each day saw him coping with longer and longer periods with less and less mechanical breathing assistance. A few days before the end of his stay in the ICU, we came in to find that the tube in his throat had been replaced by a small plaster – and that was the end of that phase. We were now well on the way to leaving Zero behind.

The next hurdle was Ben's feeding. He was still fed through a nasal gastric tube, and a young doctor new to us on the ICU told me Ben had three days to start taking liquid by mouth or they would need to fit a PEG (percutaneous endoscopic gastrostomy – a tube straight to his stomach from outside his abdomen) to support his feeding. It soon became clear he was not familiar with Ben's case and that his goal was totally unachievable. However, our anxiety about Ben meeting this three-day deadline was interpreted by staff as us having unrealistic expectations together with an unhelpful objection to the surgical intervention needed to fit the PEG. This taught us to always clarify with staff and summarise our understanding of any information we'd been given, so we could be confident we had understood and didn't feel we had to blame staff or be seen as hampering any procedure to support Ben's progress. The fact that these little setbacks seemed so awful at the time highlights how fragile and vulnerable we still were.

Now breathing on his own, but with his nasal tube still in place, Ben was transferred from the ICU to his new ward, in neuro-rehab. After the light, spacious and airy ICU, the most noticeable feature of the rehab wards was the lack of light. The long, dark corridors with wards on one side and individual rooms on the other, the staff desk positioned in the corridor outside the individual rooms and wards, offering no sight of patients, all came as a shock to me as we walked alongside Ben's bed, accompanying him down into the bowels of the hospital. He was placed in a bed on a ward with a number of other patients. He had been on a ward in the ICU but the bays there were big and the beds all faced the central staff desk.

The neuro-rehab nursing and care team were unaware of Ben's restlessness and the fact he'd been in a low bed, almost on the floor, for the past three weeks. We could sense Ben was overwhelmed by the change and we left him that first night with feelings of dread and worry. The change in setting was huge and those early feelings of high anxiety were there again but without the sense of confidence that we were leaving him in good hands.

By the morning, with Ben having had little sleep and the night staff telling us with some dismay that he'd been very restless and unsafe in his bed, they had placed him on the floor and within sight of the ward door, which gave a better view from the corridor but not the staff desk. By the next night, he'd been transferred to a single room with a care assistant allocated to him to ensure he was safe – as he became more mobile, without yet being steady on his feet, getting himself out of bed and falling was a real possibility. Later, as he became stronger and more steady, the likelihood of his wandering off and getting confused was also a risk that needed managing. This meant that the provision of care staff, often from an agency, became a feature of his time on this ward.

No phase ever seemed to last long, and in time the essential PEG was fitted. After a few weeks on a new feeding regime, Ben moved on to the next stage of his eating and drinking, with the support of a great speech and language therapist who worked expertly with him on this. Flavoured and thickened gels to reduce the chance of choking until swallowing had been relearned were introduced and gradually thinned to the point where he could manage regular drinks. He then began to master thickened and highly calorific desserts before managing puréed foods, until he could chew and manage textures. This progression was similar to that of a baby being weaned onto solid food. In the weeks that followed, he rediscovered his love of food and put on the 20kg he had lost over his two-and-a-half months of hospitalisation. He regained a healthy appetite, though with some noticeably changed preferences: he had acquired a really sweet tooth.

The routine of the rehab ward was very different from what we were used to, and Ben now had a weekly programme of physiotherapy, speech and language therapy, and occupational therapy. Within days of being in this new environment, Ben was placed in a hoist and, with the amazing support and encouragement of a fantastic physiotherapist, he took his first supported steps and made it down the length of the physio gym and back again.

This was a giant step forward. Hugh was the first to witness it, and there were tears streaming down his face as he told me in a strained voice of this momentous 'leap'. The emotion in his voice has remained a lasting memory of the pain and worry we were carrying. The care staff, too, acknowledged that it had been a momentous event.

I felt elated, hopeful and amazed at Ben's determination. I was also incredulous. This had happened so quickly. It was the beginning of an intensive programme that had him developing head control and trunk control, walking unaided, managing steps and leaving the hospital two months later with enough physical skills and strength to transfer to a home-based physio programme. It was the start of a journey with an unknown itinerary.

If one of us visited during one of Ben's physio sessions, we would sit and watch. Hugh, who always made the morning visits, got to do this most often. With humour and persistence, Ben's physiotherapist put him through his paces, pushing him on, making demands of him, but always understanding of the impact of Ben's injury on his movement. This helped to ensure he progressed at quite a pace. I marvelled at how he responded to her touch and how he followed strings of complex instructions about his position, his weight-bearing, his hips, what to push against while holding his head up and putting his arms down. She explained about muscle memory but was also hopeful that his ability to follow complex instructions with several parts was a good sign. Ben worked well with her and made rapid progress, which I think was rewarding for both of them.

In between these sessions, the care staff would walk him up and down the rehab ward's corridor, stopping to say hello to passing staff, patients or visitors, or going out into the garden, despite it being winter. Ben was like a toddler wanting to practise his walking and, though often tired, would show determination and keep going at a point where others would have to call a halt to avoid exhaustion. The staff were delighted by the progress he was making. I guess Ben's age and the nature of his injury made this very different from the progress of many elderly stroke patients on the ward. Their celebration was always uplifting and a fantastic welcome when I arrived for the twice-daily visit. It was also at odds with the feedback we got from the ward consultant, who never expressed anything that we could be positive about. That spontaneous sharing of success in front of Ben always made us glow and was something we could pass on to those who regularly asked how he was doing. Now, with hindsight, I realise these must have seemed like very small steps to those who still imagined Ben as he was before the accident. But for us, our daily experience was becoming the new normality.

Ben never liked the wheelchair, and now his returning mobility gave him even more of an excuse not to use it. When we took him to the hospital cafeteria for a change of scene, he would try to get out of the wheelchair and sit in a normal chair like the rest of us. (We complied once he was strong enough to do so.) He would also get very annoyed that he could only have his thickened drinks and not a normal drink like the rest of us. While his irritation was obvious, we also saw this as a positive sign of his growing awareness and strong determination to move on.

Ben was remarkably sensitive to how people were with him. He responded best with those he came to trust, such as his therapists or the care staff he saw often. There were times when his life became stressful, even within the routines and confines of his ward. He would panic and sometimes lash out if people he didn't know approached him without care or preparation. Ben became seen as aggressive, but no one ever connected it to how he was handled. They just saw it as part of him, and there was no effort to treat him with more understanding. The patients on the ward were mainly elderly people recovering from strokes. There wasn't much expertise on head injuries.

Once, a member of the care staff threatened to file a complaint against Ben for assault, after Ben had lashed out at him. We were mortified that anyone could make that kind of complaint on a brain injury ward. We later discovered, from a staff member who knew Ben well, that Ben had been woken up first thing in the morning by an unfamiliar person in an unfamiliar way. It was more likely he was frightened than aggressive. It was distressing all round, particularly when the medics saw it only as a symptom of the impact of his brain injury. It was seen as more evidence of his brain damage and as confirmation that we shouldn't get over-excited about Ben's possible trajectory.

Despite the extent of his head injury, there remained a logic to Ben's reasoning that was often surprising and spot-on. He started questioning parts of his occupational therapy programme: for example, teaching him to make toast, which he couldn't eat as he was still on a liquid diet; getting him ready for bed when it wasn't bed time; having a wash and cleaning his teeth when he had already done this when he got up. He also complained about being assessed. He said to me one day, 'She knows I can't do this, so I don't know why she needs me to do it again.'

His questioning was amazing to us, when this expression of quite complex language had been preceded a few weeks before by soft twitterings we couldn't understand, followed by clearer individual words, and on to short sentences that led sometimes to comments that would make us laugh, such as finding his afternoon tea quite refreshing or requesting that we bring him a salmon smoothie. And from this to his questioning of activities that expressed some illogicality.

He didn't always take to some of the practice he had to do for his fine motor skills, such as placing little pegs into small holes, or fitting a mix of peg shapes into their matching holes. I'm sure if the purpose of some of these activities had been explained to him and linked to the skills they were helping him to strengthen, he would have been more likely to see the point. He even turned his occupational therapist's name, Uta, into a verb, and would term any waste-of-time process as being 'Utared'. In fact, Ben still has the most difficulty with fine motor skills.

Evening and weekend visits became more and more crowded and, thankfully, noisy and joyous, as friends came to visit, often in groups of various sizes, crammed into Ben's small room. Walking down the long and gloomy corridor and hearing laughter, sometimes with accompanying music, was, I think, not only welcomed by us but also by others on the ward, whether they were working or visiting. Sometimes we got to Ben's room and it was empty, as friends had taken him for a bit of a wheel-about in his chair. The staff never complained about the noise or the numbers – maybe they, too, liked the life it brought to the rehab floor. Relatives of other patients joined in with positive comments, and would sometimes pop their heads around the door to take in the scene. Friends would leave their written comments in the visitors' book we'd started. The effort people made, and their support of Ben, was support for us, too. Some friends, however, found the change in Ben too distressing and only became more frequent visitors once he was home.

At this stage, Ben couldn't tell us who had visited and sometimes he would deny he'd had any visitors at all! So the visitors' book was helpful and gave us a talking point. Photographs friends brought of past events, stag dos, weddings and parties went up on the wall. We would ask Ben to name the individuals in these group photos, as there were many people we didn't know, and this became one of the various things we did routinely with him and which he showed no sign of finding tedious. I now think it's likely he didn't remember we'd already done it before and so he always got involved as if for the first time.

We always made sure a family member got Ben ready for bed, as one would a young child, with wash routines, changing into pyjamas and having some chill time before the night-time carer came on duty. I think the staff appreciated this, as it meant one less patient for them to deal with, and we did it because it meant we could leave him feeling settled. The night team were agency staff. Some we took to more than others, and some seemed pleased to be assigned to Ben, leaving us reassured.

This was a period when many healthcare scandals were being reported in the news, including national outrage over the poor treatment of elderly people in hospital. We understood completely. Our experience made us realise the problem wasn't confined to the elderly but was a much broader issue, irrespective of age. Anyone who was vulnerable – whether because of a stroke, a head injury or any other condition that made them totally dependent on staff – was at risk, particularly if they weren't visited regularly by those who knew them well. We knew that overstretched, often poorly qualified staff managing patients who could be a challenge might easily succumb to unacceptable conduct towards those who could neither speak out or defend themselves. We were no different from others who had loved ones on the ward and who stayed long hours beside their relatives to make sure they ate and drank, had access to bedpans and were toileted or changed as needed.

Thank goodness, then, for those unforgettable and priceless individuals who make all the difference. I'm sure there must be countless such people in all our hospitals. For us this was two women who, through their work as care staff, had become good friends and mostly worked shifts together. They'd worked there for a long time and, despite their officially junior positions, were pivotal in the running of the ward. They worked so hard, spreading themselves ever more thinly by going beyond the extra mile. They would pop into Ben's room briefly on their way to and fro along the corridor and, if they were able to stay a little longer, provided reassurance if it was needed. They knew his programme and wider timetable. They enjoyed spending time with him and he with them. They laughed and joked, and we could always leave it with them if a care issue needed sorting out. They became known to us as the 'duo of one'.

On more than one occasion they phoned us on a weekend day to say they were undermanned and to ask whether we were able to come in for the day as Ben didn't have his allotted care staff. This was okay, as we would rather Ben was properly cared for, and it was good they felt they could ask without difficult repercussions from us and with some certainty we would agree. However, it also meant our much-needed break, allowing us part of the day to do other things, had to be sacrificed. What would have happened if we weren't close at hand or couldn't change our plans? More to the point, it showed how very stretched and strained the whole system was, if it had to resort to the support and input of families when there was insufficient capacity to run the ward.

Miles, a friend from Bath University

As a close university friend, I was one of the few people outside Ben's family who was allowed to go and see him once he had been flown back to England.

Seeing him for the first time was incredibly nerve-wracking. In fact, visiting him was always nerve-wracking, as you never knew how he would be. A lot of my anxiety was about my own reaction and whether or not this would upset him. Looking back, there wasn't much point in being nervous as he doesn't really remember any of it anyway. What I remember most was how big and shiny his face was and how tiny the rest of his body seemed, very much like Voldemort in the first *Harry Potter* film. It didn't really look anything like him, in spite of the limited physical scarring he'd suffered.

In the earliest stages he looked to be in a lot of discomfort, stuck in a bed, semi-conscious, moving as though he was having a bad dream. It was tough to watch – an incredibly helpless feeling.

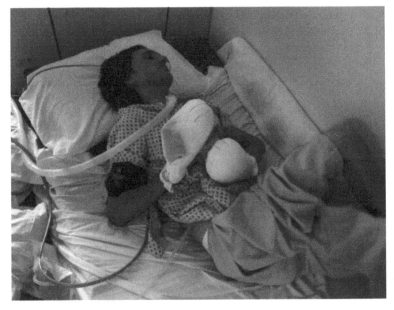

Ben in ICU in the UK, 28 October 2010

Initially, you cling to anything positive and you really reach out to make something from nothing. A movement that was just a reflex would be seized upon as some kind of acknowledgement or response to something I'd said or done, but in those days I didn't truly believe that was the case.

Then, slowly, things changed. He was waking up and almost becoming reborn. The way he has recovered and the speed with which he has gone from nothing to becoming a man again is like he almost had a second, hyper development, especially at the beginning – learning to walk and talk, the way his brain was reconnecting. Suddenly we were talking to him and playing catch with squishy balls, and then he was walking around. At one stage he would get the giggles at nothing in particular and laugh uncontrollably until it looked like it hurt a little. I can't remember how long it lasted. It was hilarious.

Ben

When I was in the ICU, my family began to keep notes of their visits – scribbled on sheets of paper and pinned to the walls. It was a way of tracking my progress and, perhaps, of reminding the nursing staff to keep their eye on the ball.

Here is a partial transcript of what they wrote, to give an impression of the level of response from me that was significant to them at the time.

The October Diary

Monday, 11 October

11.45am-12.20pm. Eyes open for 30 seconds, then back to sleep. Very sleepy today. Nurse said he didn't get much sleep last night.

4pm. Surprise – physio had Ben sitting in a chair! Wow! Has managed to be off his ventilator since 10am. Very alert in terms of looking – nods or some shakes, closing eyes to questions.

Thursday, 14 October

12pm. Ben pushed his right leg on request three times in succession. He poked his tongue out (a little bit) on request! He then fell asleep.

Friday, 15 October

11am-1pm. Eyes open and very alert. He gave us a little smile, raised his eyebrows when showed pictures of university, and other, friends. He gave us a nod when we asked if he wanted the headphones in both ears. The most active I've seen him so far!

Thursday, 21 October

11.30am. Quite active and alert. Physio session, then put in the chair. Did the crossword with him — looked closely and seemed interested, then fell asleep.

Friday, 22 October

11.30pm. Very awake and lots of movements, arms and legs, he kicked me in the face. A few eyebrow raises. Lots of movement with legs.

Evening visit. Very focused on the South Park *DVD for a good 15 minutes — a number of expressions and legs restless while he watched. Opening his mouth and biting his oxygen monitor!*

Sunday, 24 October (Week 5 today)

Morning visit. Managed to twist himself right around the bed. When I arrived his head was on the floor and feet over the end! On 24hr 'trachy' (tracheostomy) mask. Has been quite sleepy but moments of good, focused looking — some relevant nodding. Left him sitting in chair and watching Family Guy.

Evening. Sleepy then more and more alert. Listened to tapes made by Andy and Caspar. Noticed his left knee was bruised so asked him if he hit it on the bed — he nodded.

Tuesday, 26 October

Looked in the mirror for the first time. I think he was happy with what he saw.

Thursday, 28 October

Afternoon. Licked his lips when discussing smoked salmon. Watched 10–15 min of Family Guy. *Looked at Indonesian photos — very focused. Still very restless.*

Sunday, 31 October

We sat Ben up on the edge of the bed twice — he tried to stand but we stopped him. Responded to lots of questions. Kissed his mother twice, once on request.

Afternoon. Sat him up on the edge of bed for a few minutes, lots of leg exercises, supported my whole body weight with his legs. Awake the whole time. Was tired at the beginning. He gave me and Naomi a kiss on demand when we were saying goodbye.

Evening. Took three very small spoonfuls of water. A very little cough with the first and clear swallow with second and third. Opened his mouth on request and swallowed. Sat on the edge of bed twice – responded to request to sit up straight, lifting his head – having clearly nodded that he wanted to sit up. Nodded to say he wanted to listen to another chapter of The Hitchhiker's Guide to the Galaxy *– seemed focused and remained alert for 30 mins. Still quite restless – from side-to-side. More low 'soft' noises. Kisses us goodbye consistently now!*

November 2010 Visitors' Book (Neuro-Rehabilitation Ward)

I now have in my possession 'Ben's visitors' book', a simple plain-paper notebook. On the first page is written, in my mother's handwriting, 'We've got into the habit of summarising our visits as a way of communicating between ourselves. So feel free to add your comments and let Ben know what you are writing.'

Inside is a mix of carefully written notes and hurried scribbles, in a variety of hands, in different coloured pens and, occasionally, in pencil. The notes and messages track my progress during that first month in rehab, providing a true and contemporary record of life in my individual room on the rehab ward. Here are some edited highlights.

Tuesday, 2 November

Day 2. Back in Room C. Less restless today. Sat on the edge of the bed. Seemed eager to be sitting. Turned his head to look at each of us in turn. Attentive to each of us as we spoke to him. Fell asleep.

Friday, 5 November (Bonfire Night)

Came to see you, Ben, and was excited to find you looking so great. Standing, talking and eating. Hats off to you, mate, for being so strong. Great to see you, man. Much love, Morgan X

See you again soon, man. You're a sight for sore eyes. Love James X

Hi Ben. Was great to see you. You're doing really well. Will be back soon, maybe head down with Lizzie. Love Rol XX

Sunday, 7 November

2pm. Asleep when we arrived then woke and almost jumped out of bed! We were then able to have an extended conversation with him! We could understand him and he could understand us.

Monday, 15 November

Saw Ben. Nice catch–up. Spin round hospital – all very fun. Morgan

Afternoon visit. Had a taste of smoked salmon 'paste'. Didn't go down a bundle. Successfully peed – catheter out! Hooray!

Tuesday, 16 November

Afternoon. Asleep when I arrived, then he woke. We practised making some 'whoo' noises and when he got some volume I then got him to shape the sound with lips and tongue. Succeeded very quickly in getting him to use his voice, copying short phrases after me. Reverted to whispering afterwards but it shows he can do it. It's just his general muscular weakness is the problem.

Evening visit. Found Ben in the dining room – seemed cross and agitated, swore and tried to get out of his chair. Talking more distinctly – when asked if he wanted us to bring him anything he said, 'Some ale, scotch bonnet chillies and a cocktail!' When Naomi said, 'I didn't think you liked cocktails,' he said, 'I don't!' Played some games on the iPad with Naomi. Expressed his feelings of frustration – 'It's fucking terrible. It's frustrating. Fucking awful.'

Saturday, 20 November

Morning visit from Hugh and Jenny as Ben wanted to see us after unsettling episode. Naomi and Theo visit with Billy. Long visit. Ate a Forticreme with enthusiasm.

Hugh and Jenny evening visit. Ben agitated and aggressive towards staff nurse and Hugh. Kicking, rather 'wild' look, lashed out and definitely uncharacteristic behaviour. Has been swearing and making verbal threats. Left him asleep.

Sunday, 28 November

Campbell and Theo visited at lunchtime.'Incredible progress since I (Campbell) last came. Good chat.'

Naomi

Ben's recovery was the hardest time I think we will ever go through. We all worked so hard for him – we were all there at his bedside every second we could spare.

The most distressing moment was when I found him on a mattress, on the floor, in a nappy. He had that terrified, wild look in his eyes that had been there since he'd started to become more conscious. He wasn't communicating. He was like a newborn baby. I was upset the nurse in there was just sitting looking at him while he rolled around on the mattress on the floor in a nappy. Why wasn't she interacting with him? Why was she looking at him like she didn't want to be there? I sat down on the mattress next to him, brushed his hair, chatted to him about my day, the weather. I tried to make him feel comforted and loved, not alone. As he lay next to me he started to push at me – he was pushing me away. I didn't understand why and I tried to comfort him. Then I felt something wet on my leg. He had wet himself and it had run out of his nappy onto me. I was mortified he was trying to let me know and I hadn't understood. I felt so humiliated and I was distraught for him. I struggled to tell anyone about that moment. I still find it incredibly hard just to think about it.

There were comical moments, too: him rolling over with his bum in the air to ask us if his bottom was clean; his trousers falling down around his ankles as we helped him walk along the hallway to the TV room; when he first started talking and he whispered to us his drink was 'very refreshing'. Very refreshing! Of all the things he could say, after not uttering a word for months. It seemed so inspired – he was only talking about a sip of water he'd just had! Then there was Ben telling the nurses he had pet koalas at home. And at home, after being discharged from hospital and the rehab nurses had finished, when he introduced Miles to one of his friends from his time at LSE (the London School of Economics) and explained, 'Miles used to be my friend but now he fucks my sister.' The hysteria these events brought on was uncontrollable – you need to find something to laugh about in such dark times, and when they happen, boy, you laugh the hardest you think you've ever laughed.

Ben

While I was in hospital, the people around me were all I knew and the only 'normal' I could relate to. While I knew it wasn't the home or life I had come from, it was my reality – the only reality I could relate to. I didn't have any memory of what my life was like. In this state all I wanted was to feel normal again and to feel I had a safe environment around me. I knew people would come and make sure I'd been to the toilet and others would come and get me to do things that were difficult and hard work – and why the hell was I doing them?

I had a strict regime of physio that was supposed to get my muscles moving again in the ways they used to but couldn't remember. I had to get some exercise but it was extremely hard. I had to walk and I knew I could walk and had walked before, so why couldn't I walk again right now? I was so unsteady on my feet, I needed someone to guide me and help me – I couldn't do it by myself. When people gave me clear instructions, then things were better. There was some reasoning behind why I was standing up and what I needed to do to be able to sit down again. I just had to follow what people were saying to me – *move over here and move this leg here.*

These were things I tried and tried to do, but my body just wouldn't follow the commands. I needed to do things I could do before and I was driven by knowing I had done them. The physio was key to this. I was made to do things that were difficult, to get my body to do movements it had forgotten how to do. As I had been in a coma for a month, it was struggling to find the strength to work as it used to. All the time in hospital I had to do things that were extremely difficult and that my body had got out of the habit of doing.

Also, I had lost so much weight – about half what I weighed

before the accident – and I was desperately trying to regain it. However, for a long time I was not given proper food to eat as I was fed through the naso-gastric tube I was wired up to. This meant I was given drips that fed me nutrients and saline solutions through cannulas to keep me hydrated and give my body the energy it needed. I had to learn to eat real food again slowly, over time. It was all so hard.

'Home?'

When Ben came home, those first few months were difficult. But of course we would not have had it any other way. We wanted him home again.

Naomi Clench, Ben's sister

*

Jenny

Throughout Ben's time in rehab, the goal was to get him home. We set ourselves the target of Ben being home for Christmas. Naomi asked how we would manage Christmas if he was still in hospital and we said that, of course, if we needed to, we would bring Christmas to him. But we saw no reason why he couldn't be home either for the day or, even better, for the Christmas and New Year period.

We shared this at the group meeting in November. Group meetings were monthly gatherings of all those involved in Ben's care and rehabilitation, including ourselves and Ben, to provide feedback on achievements to date and to agree therapy aims for the next month. Chaired by the neuro-rehab ward consultant, whose people and communication skills were disappointingly poor, these were not the meetings they could have been – so different from those feedback sessions we'd had all those weeks ago in the Dominican Republic. We'd been spoiled by knowing what 'good' felt like in these awful and difficult situations.

When we said we wanted Ben home for Christmas, there were several sharp intakes of breath around the room. People exchanged glances or looked away, and we were told this would need time and planning, with home assessments from the occupational therapists and full risk assessments to be carried out before any home visit. Well, that was fine, we thought. We'd given them more than a month to put it all in motion. The consultant, while not happy, gave his consent for the processes to be put in place. We decided to keep quiet for now about our intention to have him home through to New Year.

The first day-visits home took place at weekends. We left the hospital armed with all the information about what consistency his food had to be, how to avoid any choking and how to flush his PEG to avoid any build-up of bacteria. He had been weighed by the nutritionist to make sure the home visits didn't result in any weight-loss. On that first visit, Ben – dressed in his coat, hat and gloves for the first time that winter – was waiting for us, all ready in his chair, in the stifling heat of the ward. We wheeled him down the corridor and into the lift. He had learned to touch the right button, with a prompt, to take us to the exit, and out we whooshed with a spring in our step.

We both could have kicked our heels together with a leap in the air like in some big production musical, spinning Ben's wheelchair through the entrance and shouting to the general public that we were going home. We fitted the wheelchair in the back of the car and set off, Ben strapped in the back between Naomi and myself.

The one piece of information we could really have done with was some warning about the possibility of car sickness. The overwhelming effect of the motion, speed and perceptual confusion on Ben's senses was something neither he nor we were prepared for, and at one point we had to quickly stop the car as he thought he might vomit, before continuing the journey with his head in his sister's lap and the reassurance we were nearly home. This was the most alarming feature of the first journeys home and revealed an important gap in all the information we'd been given, as we later learned car sickness isn't uncommon after a brain injury. In fact, no one was at all surprised when we told them what had happened. Sitting Ben in the front on future journeys made it easier, and eventually this was no longer an issue.

At this stage Ben was walking short distances, with us following close behind or holding his elbows to correct and support his unsteady gait. The repeated refrain of 'Where's Ben?' would have us leaping up to check where he had got to. His breathing was noisy and rasping so we usually found him by listening for the sound. Nowhere was out of bounds. Why would it be? This was his home. But he had little sense of possible danger from falls, and in a split second seemed able to scarper off about the house. Occasionally he managed to climb the stairs. Up was no problem. However, coming down made us nervous until he was safely back on the ground floor. He could sit in a chair with good posture but needed some help getting on and off the sofa, as it was a little lower than the height of his hospital bed. He could drink and eat puréed food and drink without help though he still needed help managing in the loo.

These early visits gave us a glimpse of what we had to look forward to, as well as the realisation of the continued input he would need, both from a specialist therapy team and ourselves. However, the visits provided us with a chink of light at the end of the tunnel of nightmare. We saw an end to his hospital stay and we were all convinced the best place for him, and for the next phase of his recovery, would be home.

Ben

When I made that first visit 'home', to be re-introduced to my parents' house, it was very strange. I was going back to the place I'd lived for most of my life yet, even though there was this deep connection, I could not remember it. My memory had been so seriously wiped that memories had to be consciously relived before I could remember them. This made me extremely worried about going back to my house because it was something I could not imagine. Re-entering the house was scary. I knew it should be familiar but it wasn't. At this point in my recovery the only thing 'normal' was the hospital. Anything outside it, I simply did not know and I was scared at the prospect of re-engaging with a life I'd forgotten. With no memories to enrich my understanding of the world, my reality was based on the immediate. Life in hospital was the only reality I knew, and anything outside it was unknown. While I accepted that the people around me were my parents or family members, the experience was clouded in a deep uncertainty.

I remember it was December and coming up to Christmas time when I was first able to leave hospital to go home, initially just for a day to get used to it. It was the first time I'd been out of hospital since I arrived, and my first glimpse of other parts of my life again. I sat in the back of my parents' car as we drove away from the hospital, and the motion made me feel incredibly sick, to the point where I demanded my dad stop the car as I thought I was going to throw up. On top of this I was terribly nervous at leaving the hospital and going home to a world I didn't know. This was the first big leap into the unknown – but there would be many more to come.

My parents have reminded me that I also came home for a whole weekend but I was exceptionally anxious to get back to hospital by the end of it. I guess it had become a safe place for me – I knew it well and my routine was more familiar there. Going home was a daunting prospect, full of unknowns. But my family tell me that after staying at home the second time, for Christmas, I did not want to go back to hospital, even though I had to in order to be formally discharged. This shows how confused I was about not remembering home yet being anxious to rediscover it. It was such a disorientating experience to go through. Imagine not remembering anything about your life. The fact that my memories did begin to come back was marvellous; otherwise my recovery would have been a far worse experience and it would have been even more difficult for me to pick up my life again.

Naomi

When Ben came home, those first few months were difficult. Adjusting to life at home was tricky. There were bells on Ben's bedroom door so we could hear if he got up in the night to go to the loo and make sure he didn't fall down the stairs. But of course we would not have had it any other way. We wanted him home again.

And there was Ben's anger. It started when he was still in hospital, and you would never know when it was coming. It could be quite distressing: he kicked Miles when he wouldn't take him home with him – he wanted to go home! At other times it seemed random and passed quickly. At home, however, I found the anger difficult and, if I'm honest, I think it pushed Theo and me away. Our relationship with him still suffers because of it. We knew Ben couldn't help it, but it was hard to take. When you think you're going to lose someone and you put so much time, energy and love into them, only to be rejected and feel like nothing you do is ever good enough, that instead it always makes them angry, it's hurtful as well as exhausting.

Ben still gets very angry with me. It often comes out of nowhere and I have no idea what I've done to cause such upset. It distresses me. I feel as though I can never get it right with him, so sometimes it's easier to remove myself from the situation completely. I sometimes talk to Mum and Theo about how he's reverted to a kind of adolescence – that rage you have as a teenager, always bubbling under the surface ready to explode at any time. I don't think all that negativity I sense from Ben can be a positive thing for us as a family or, most importantly, for him.

Theo and I didn't live at home so we had an escape, but for me this came with an overwhelming sense of guilt. At first it was about not being there every weekend, but then we accepted we had to live our own lives again. And then it became about Mum and Dad having to deal with his rage every day and me feeling pleased not to be there, constantly on the receiving end. I still live with a lot of guilt about that.

Jenny

Towards the end of Ben's second day-visit home, he was sitting quietly on the sofa, the weak afternoon light fading, and in a small voice he asked no one in particular to take him 'home'. I remember the exchange of looks between his dad and me. Shock-horror that his world had become so shrunken. That look also conveyed a sign to stay silent and not to show our dismay that his family home meant no more to him than a place away from what he was now so familiar with. It made us realise how institutionalised he'd become and how the small space of his hospital room must have made him feel secure. We never seriously felt this was a rejection of home but it made us realise how draining new experiences must be for him, how much they took out of him and the effort needed for everything he did.

Nonetheless, we felt the stimulation of home would give him far greater variety and different challenges, which were more likely to push him and allow him to set his own limits that we could then respond to. We established with the hospital staff that we wanted him discharged and thus home permanently in the New Year.

Having had agreement from the rehab team that he could be home over the Christmas period, we asked the staff how we should handle socialising. Their advice was to make sure Ben wasn't overwhelmed or put into confusing situations with large groups where he was likely to find it difficult to make sense of conversations if people were all talking at once. With that warning lodged in our minds, we started our Christmas together, reunited at home as a family for the first time in many months.

The tradition of Christmas homecoming among his friends continues to bring them back to Brighton, from wherever they have settled, in time for the traditional get-together on Christmas Eve. That year, with Ben having arrived home from hospital that day, it was decided among his friends that the usual gathering would start at our house around Ben. I still remember our living room crammed with 15-20 of Ben's 'home crowd', those who'd grown up with him and cemented long and enduring friendships at college before going off to university. Ben was sitting on the sofa looking somewhat bemused, surrounded by friends keen to re-acquaint themselves with him. He was somewhat overwhelmed but obviously pleased that Christmas, or at least something different, was happening and had started off by coming to him. How fantastic! Here was the bunch of mates who had sent the messages and songs played to Ben in those early days. Some had got together quite often to share news and provide each other with support while Ben's life hung on a thread. Some had been visitors to the hospital in the evenings or at weekends and, of course, for some this was the first time they'd seen him since his accident. There was only a small voice of caution, way back in the recesses of my mind, to remind me of the advice the hospital had given us earlier that day. But on that occasion, Ben remained calm and appeared pleased to have such merriment around him.

Friends bring their Christmas gathering to Ben, December 2010

Over the next few weeks and months, our role as parents and close family changed. In those early days, when Ben's friends took him out with them, I felt like an overly fussy mother leaving them in charge of a young child, assuming they had no experience of very young children – well, they had no experience of this much-changed Ben. We would exchange mobile numbers, checking where they were going and roughly when they planned to be back. It was easier when these exchanges still took place during the picking-up and dropping-off from home, with Ben compliant and accepting that this was now a set routine before leaving the house with friends. It was a whole different ball game when he became more independent and started to come and go without us always knowing where he was or who he was with, and with no means of contacting him.

Hugh

Inevitably there were physical challenges at home that Ben hadn't had to face in hospital. Our rather old and tatty stair carpet, which we'd lived with for nearly 20 years, had lots of loose ends that might trip Ben up, so we replaced it with something new and better fitted. In any case, for months I would walk in front of, or behind, him whenever he went up or down the stairs, in case he tripped, as he remained very unsteady on his feet for quite some time.

We put Ben in the bedroom right next to us, which had been his in the dim, distant past, and while we no longer had to worry about whether he was comfortable before going to sleep, we were soon very worried about his nocturnal excursions, which would usually wake us with a loud crashing sound as he fell over in the dark. In hospital he had been supervised, with somebody in his room throughout the night, no doubt for the same reason.

This situation caused us great anxiety and we slept very badly. After a few sleepless nights I rigged up a Heath Robinson-style alarm system connecting Ben's door to ours using cord and porcelain runners, so when he opened his door it would raise a decorative metal contraption with bells on it, suspended inside our bedroom door. Unfortunately, we soon discovered the bells were not always loud enough to wake us, so I took to balancing short pieces of wood on the door's metalwork, which would clatter to the floor and wake us unfailingly.

Nonetheless, this was all vastly preferable to driving out to the hospital three times a day, and after several weeks' delay following Ben's permanent return home he began receiving three daily visits from Social Services carers. This was standard practice to support people leaving hospital who were unable to care for themselves. However, they all refused to supervise him on the stairs as I did, apparently because of health and safety regulations. We never did quite understand the rationale of this – presumably it was to safeguard the worker, as it certainly wasn't in the interest of the client. So, although their presence provided us with a modicum of respite, we still had to be alert to see what the carers were up to and to keep an eye on them.

The worst thing was the lack of continuity in his carers, some of whom appeared to be in need of care themselves. Certainly, a few seemed to be lacking in any common sense and it often seemed these visits were more trouble than they were worth. Despite this criticism, Social Services has undoubtedly been the best and most helpful resource in supporting Ben since he arrived back in the UK after his accident.

Jenny

We learned from the hospital social worker that, on discharge from the hospital, help was at hand. Assessments both in hospital and at home had identified Ben as being eligible for home support, which meant visits from the disability home visiting team, a specialist community service within adult social care. We knew we had to have this type of support for at least a month, which was deemed long enough to demonstrate that it wasn't ideal in supporting Ben's recovery and that the alternative solution, of direct payments from Social Services that Ben could use to arrange his own care and support, would be preferable. So for a month the 30-minute visits at 8am, midday and 8pm, while gratefully received, formed yet another routine we were shoehorned into. The times were specifically selected so the carers could help get Ben up, assist him at lunchtime in the preparation of meals, and put him to bed. I think other visit times were discussed, but these seemed to make most sense.

If you were living on your own and had no other way of getting up or feeding yourself, I can see this service would be a lifeline. One carer was very good at ensuring Ben made his bed, something that had not been part of his routine for the past ten years, but he was very obliging. (He has now reverted to the old habit of not making his bed!) At midday, however, unless Ben knew what he might want for lunch, with the ingredients out and ready, the half-hour was always rushed. It was best suited to reheating prepared meals, which meant I had to be organised before leaving for work and leave something out. Even simple meals like cheese on toast, following Ben's explanation of how he wanted it, could end up being an unusual version involving the scraping of melted cheese off a metal tray from under the grill onto a piece of toast. I don't think this spoiled Ben's enjoyment of his lunch but it did take us a while to persuade him there was a simpler way of making cheese on toast with equally good, if not better, results. It soon became clear that having so many different strangers carrying out these personal and domestic tasks, at times that didn't always fit in with him or us, was never going to be the ideal solution to providing the right care and support.

We stuck with it for the required month, until something different could be offered. We cancelled visits if we knew they weren't going to fit in with our day, and nearly always cancelled the evening visit as Ben wasn't ready to go to bed at eight. The weekend visit we also cancelled, preferring to pass on the early-morning wake-up. However, the knock on the door first thing on a Saturday morning, or when we were still sitting at supper, would make me groan, as we realised we'd forgotten to cancel and a wasted trip had been made.

The carers were always courteous and smiling, however, never letting any irritation show if it was clear they weren't needed. I hope it at least gave them a little more slack on their rounds, as their timetable for visits was always tight and never afforded any leeway. I felt bad for wasting scarce resources but Ben's lovely social worker thought our ever-changing needs only bolstered Ben's application for funds to arrange his own bespoke and flexible support.

Ben's return home also meant a transfer of his hospital therapy programme for the following four months to a multidisciplined specialist community rehabilitation team, who could visit Ben at home throughout the week. The therapists each liaised with Ben and us during their visits if they needed to, but also at monthly team meetings, at home, where we agreed on goals that combined Ben's own aspirations with an integrated common approach, shared between the different disciplines, which linked his speech, occupational and physio therapies. We had hoped the dreaded format of the hospital meetings would be an experience we'd never need to suffer again, but eventually, with some adjustment to the roles of certain professionals, we achieved a better understanding and some good outcomes.

Everyday living skills, such as shopping, cooking and using public transport, were Jo's domain. Jo was an experienced support worker who worked closely with all the therapists, putting their recommended activities for Ben into the context of daily life. So Ben and Jo took buses into town and went for coffee to give the journey purpose. It helped Ben to learn how to handle money again, to choose the best seat on the bus, and ask the driver to give him time to sit down before the bus moved off. They would also go to the corner shop with a list I'd drawn up of a few basics needed for his lunch.

The home physiotherapy programme branched out to the park, swimming pool and eventually the local gym. Speech therapy focused on Ben developing more language skills – rediscovering nouns, for example, and learning to organise his thinking. He began to read again and, with great effort, his writing slowly came back. He was asked to keep a daily diary to support this, but this became such a struggle he no longer wanted to do it. The occupational therapist would help to find solutions to daily challenges, such as special pens to help with Ben's grip and mobile phones simple enough to get him back into technology.

The comings and goings of the community rehab team worked well over the next few months, but while they were taking care of Ben's physical ability, we were anxious to see him become more 'himself' again in other ways, too. To help him re-connect with the emotional and social aspects of his identity, we did one of the most rewarding and worthwhile things of all. At the suggestion of the community speech therapist, we made a time-line.

We covered two long walls in the dining room with lining paper and sectioned it off into chunks of Ben's life: before university, time at university, and his later life in London living on his narrowboat, leading to his early working life. Inadvertently, this provided a way to show how the various groups of Ben's friends related to the different phases of his life. These friends tended to visit Ben at home together and had lots of things in common to share and remember, which they started to add to the timeline. Dates, events, drawings, messages and photographs soon began to fill what had once been virginally white sheets. The timeline also brought an ease to the visits. The talk and banter around memories for the timeline didn't demand that Ben remember them, and removed any need for him to initiate the conversation, which he wasn't capable of doing. Most importantly, it included him in a relaxed way, while the flowing talk and laughter brought some joy into the house, which was welcomed all round.

Ben's memory wall in 2011, also known as his timeline and 'the wall

'The wall', as we called it, grew and grew and changed with every visit in Ben's early months at home. It became an expectation that every visitor add their bit before leaving. It evolved into the most marvellous piece of house graffiti, something that could not be ignored by anyone coming into the house. It was a backdrop to our mealtimes. It surrounded us as Ben's home therapy meetings took place, giving us a sense that life was rich and Ben's networks were strong and healthy and alive beyond the world of therapists. It added colour and an originality which we grew to love. It impressed friends and family who hadn't been involved in its growing.

After several months, perhaps almost six, it became a fixture we lived with comfortably and in time nothing further was added. This probably coincided with Ben socialising more and more outside the home. We still enjoyed its intricacies, the image it gave of his life before the accident. It also provided Ben with an easy prompt to talk about events and people he still needed a nudge to place and remember. It remained a point of conversation, which helped him initiate discussion and ask questions. Generating original questions remained really difficult for him for a long time but, as he gazed across this wonderful thing, it set his memory cogs whirring and, of course, also gave more topics to draw out of him.

I can't remember at what point it came down. Another stage had been reached and passed.

Ben

My experience of going home left me in a quagmire of unsettling discontent. People who visited and talked to me said they had known me for years, or were part of my family, but I couldn't be certain it was true because it relied on my brain working properly, something I couldn't have any faith in.

I've been told since that my memory of places I'd been to was quite accurate even early on, and I even told Miles and Campbell I'd been to the Dominican Republic and Haiti, which is why I was in hospital. They said they didn't know how to take this, as maybe it meant I remembered Jazz. This wasn't cleared up until after I left hospital, when I finally asked my parents, 'Did I have a girlfriend?' They later told me they'd been dreading this question. When they answered me, 'Yes, you had a girlfriend called Jazz. She died in the accident', my initial response was that because I didn't remember her, I wasn't going to pursue it any further. I was already so overwhelmed by all the things I was doing in order to get well.

But the fact I couldn't remember her annoyed me and made me constantly question the validity of my brain. *Why can't I remember her? For this reason, how can I trust anything? There are things I am supposed to remember but I can't. These people say they are my parents, but I don't really know who they are.* There was no certainty in my memory, and there was so much going on that didn't prompt any recollection.

This phase of my recovery was riddled with uncertainty. I was losing faith in my own abilities to understand who I was. There is nothing worse you can lose than your sense of self. Losing all ability to know who you are is about as difficult as it gets.

To counteract this mental fluidity, I took control of my own care as far as I could. I had some involvement by having my say with certain members of the community rehab team when their involvement became counter-productive to the way I accessed the therapies. There was one woman who was a psychologist and the keyworker for the team. She took it upon herself to talk for me at the weekly team meetings, speaking with an air of authority, saying *Ben thinks this...* or *He thinks that...* I soon said this was ridiculous, as she never spent any time with me except at these meetings, when she assumed the role of mouthpiece and spoke as though she had consulted me on whatever form she thought the care should take. I became extremely agitated about this and told the other members of the team, asking how dare she speak for me when she never spent any time with me. She claimed I was unnecessarily angry and she warned me at one of the team meetings that support would be withdrawn if I continued to be disrespectful to team members. While I'm sure I used bad language about her to those who worked with me, no one else ever made any complaints about me during their therapy sessions with me.

This woman's only direct involvement with me had been when she assessed my mood before the community rehab team became involved in my home therapy programme, which I assume was to see if I was depressed, which I wasn't. She produced a questionnaire full of leading questions such as, 'Do you sometimes feel worthless?' and 'Do you have suicidal thoughts?' I couldn't see any relevance at all to the support I needed.

After one particularly annoying meeting, when she told me off about my use of language when discussing her with other therapists, I'd had enough. Her presence was a waste of my time and energy. I wanted a new keyworker. My parents wrote a letter, with my agreement, requesting a change of keyworker, citing my lack of rapport with this woman and frustration at not being able to get on with the rehabilitation process, and it was agreed that one of the other therapists would take on this role. I felt it was a good outcome.

It was clear my memory had been severely affected by the injury I'd suffered. To help bring back memories, including the sequence of events in my life, my parents created a map of my life that we posted up on the dining room wall at home. A very old friend of mine, Richard, from my school days, was the first person to write on it, and he helped set the tone for the other contributions, using colour and drawings and informal scribbles. He gave me a lot of help with recovering memories of my school years, and what he'd written inspired others to add to the wall. People would add to it when they came to see me, and it was a great way of getting all my friends involved in rebuilding my memory. It was a collaborative effort, with people contributing wherever they could, as there were so many parts of my life I still had no idea about. The wall became a mind-map of my life which I could refer to, and this gave me a way to re-establish the memories that should have been there.

Caroline, Ben's aunt

Shortly after Ben arrived back in England after his accident, I came to visit him in hospital. He was no longer in the intensive care unit but in a room on a ward of severe neurological trauma cases, mostly older people. There he was, propped up in his bed, the lights dimmed. He was very thin but his eyes hadn't lost their intensity. It was quite a surprise, actually, as there were no visible signs of trauma or, at least, only very slight scarring left from the lacerations of the accident. There wasn't much to do in that small room. It was a little cramped, so I sat on the bed. I asked Ben, 'Do you know who I am?' Over the course of several visits, I usually got a nod or a mumbled 'Yeah', but I wasn't too sure, so I would just touch his arm or hold his hand by way of reassurance and in acknowledgement of his response to me.

I wasn't there when Ben came out of hospital or for that first Christmas they spent together as a family again, so the next time I saw him he was sitting in the front of the car with Hugh. I'd flown in from the South of France and they'd come to collect me at the airport. Imagine the contrast! It was thrilling. It was around February and Jenny and Hugh had got things organised for Ben at home, so there we were, on our way back to normal life.

The happiness and joy of having Ben home contrasted with what was quite a stressful situation for everyone, as he would stumble around the house, not so sure of his footing. The house had a few areas that Ben was discouraged from visiting if he was alone, such as the top floor and the stairs, where he needed support. He was going through the process of starting all over again, acquiring simple skills. When he got stuck somewhere I would hear him call 'Dad!' and Hugh would arrive, patient as ever, and get him back on track. This happened so many times a day Hugh couldn't get on with his work. A number of carers and therapists came in the morning through to lunch. During that stay I tried to keep track of Ben in the afternoons, when he had nothing planned, giving Hugh a breather and the short-lived illusion he could get some work done. But, invariably, after a short while Ben would shout 'Dad!' just like a toddler and, I guess, as with a small child, it was mainly to make sure he was still there.

The house had also undergone a few transformations. The walls in the dining area were like the Bayeux Tapestry – huge sheets of paper were fixed to the walls, notes and pictures taped up on it with dates and names, Ben's life unfolded across the room to prompt his memory. There was so much I didn't know. I would sit with him and get him to tell me, *When was this?* or *Who is that?* Sometimes he would just say, 'Oh, I can't remember,' which would make us laugh, as of course I had no idea either. He would brush it off, saying, 'It's my abasanjo.' I wasn't too sure what this 'abasanjo' was. Did this refer to a blank in his memory, or was he naming his accident?

We spent lots of time together talking about the events on the memory wall and then selecting photo albums on the iPad. We looked at the pictures taken during his work in Africa; his holidays in Nigeria with a former girlfriend, Katie; his time in Thailand. But mostly pictures of Jazz. These are happy memories for me. It was such fun: he was light and bubbly at these times. He remembered so much of what we were looking at – but when it came to Jazz, there was nothing doing; he couldn't remember a thing. We probably looked at all his pictures of Jazz. There were the holidays spent in New York and Montréal with her sister, her mum with her cats – all this he remembered, but when it came to Jazz I would ask him, *Is there nothing you recall?* And there wasn't. He just said, *Whoa, was she really my girlfriend? Well, she looks great. Isn't she beautiful!* And that was it. He would move on.

One day I found him at the top of the house, looking at his bedroom, and at the bits and bobs on the shelves. 'Is this my room?' Silent moments, as he looked at his stuff, not quite sure these things were really his. He was still staying in Theo's bedroom on the lower floor, where it was more accessible, and hadn't moved back into his own room yet. So when I found him up there, sussing out his bedroom, he was most certainly not supposed to be up all those stairs alone, without help. But that is Ben: curious and not taking no for answer – *I want to see what's there, and I don't want or need anybody's help.*

Another time, I heard the most monumental crash, and there he was, sprawled out on the lower staircase. 'Ben, what are you doing?' I asked, and he answered with a laugh, as if he couldn't tell me himself how he'd got there, let alone acknowledge the fact he wasn't supposed to be near there at all.

Yes, Ben was home, and making progress all the time. To see him take up the challenge of crossing a wide space, or just making his way around a room, with his wobbly steps – the determination to get there, without necessarily appreciating the obstacles in his path – was quite a feat to admire and it most certainly was a relief when he got to the other side.

When you didn't have Ben in sight, or if you noticed a particular sort of silence in the house, you knew there could be trouble ahead. One morning, he wasn't around in the usual places, and I couldn't hear him, either. I was on alert mode as I entered his room. The curtains were still drawn and the morning light only slightly filtered through. I found Ben curled up on the bed. I was worried. As I could tell he was awake, I asked him gently, 'What's up? You don't feel well?' I was expecting an answer such as, 'I feel sick' or 'My stomach hurts.' Instead he told me he was not okay and he wasn't feeling 'all right'. I could see he was feeling lost. 'I don't know who I am,' he said.

We set off on a long and complicated conversation. Silent tears as he questioned me, saying, quite logically, if he could not remember his girlfriend, how could he be sure the two people who say they are his parents, are really his parents? He was worried. They'd told him at the hospital they were his parents; he believed them, but he couldn't remember them. 'I don't know who they really are!'

I think this was one of the most important moments I've shared with Ben. I started evoking our shared memories. He didn't doubt those, so he could accept Jenny and Hugh were, of course, his parents, just as Naomi and Theo were his siblings. If he couldn't remember Jazz right now, he would later. That's what we all thought at the time.

Jenny

It's April, six months after Ben's accident, a sunny afternoon at home and Ben has fallen asleep in the garden. He does that frequently in the first few months back home. I watch him: relaxed, breathing quietly, neither his features nor his pose and position show any signs of what he's been through. I fix this moment as a snapshot in time, consciously wondering what Ben will be like in the next few years. Will the impact of his brain injury mean he will always be seen as different? Or will he pass as one of the crowd, people seeing Ben the person first and noticing his impairment or difficulties second? But his lying there asleep gives me a glimpse of what we might be heading for along the continuum of normality. There's that too-familiar feeling of grieving for the Ben that was and will never be again, and yet still looking forward to getting on with life, hoping that eventually Ben will also get on, despite the likely obstacles, and get the best out of life.

Becoming Ben Again

Rebuilding My Body

Oh, and physically, he's run a half-marathon.

I could never run a half-marathon. Enough said.

Robbie Barkell, a friend of Ben's and Jazz's from LSE, on Ben's recovery

*

Ben

Employing Andrew as an assistant to aid me in my recovery was the best thing I could have done. I hired him just two months after getting out of hospital, even though they had told us it could take a long time to find someone. My dad found him by putting an ad on Gumtree, which got a number of responses within a couple of days.

Andrew being an independent carer meant we did things the NHS nurses would not have wanted us to do, such as going cycling. When we said we were doing this, they said they'd have to do a risk assessment on it first to make sure it was safe. However, Andrew and I didn't care about such things, so we just took my dad's bike to the park so I could get used to it again and ride as I had in the past. This was a comical sight, though, as my dad's bike saddle was far too high for me to touch the ground with both feet while in the saddle. So, as I cycled off around the park, Andrew would run along beside me in case I stopped and toppled over. I imagine this would have looked very amusing – one man wobbling along on a bike with another chasing after him.

During these trips to the park, we soon noticed there were various exercise machines there as well. We both tried them out, not really as purposeful exercise but just because it was quite good fun. In some ways, Andrew was paid by me simply to be around and help me to have fun, which we did in our own way.

Nevertheless, he made sure we did all the physical work the rehabilitation staff had set me, as well as enjoying the time we spent together.

He was around more frequently than the NHS staff, and would be there when the rehab team went through my activity programme. This involved a lot of work on my hands, in particular, because I'd suffered nerve damage that affected them. I needed to do a lot of exercises to strengthen my finger muscles so that my hands could be mobile and active. Andrew would make sure I did the exercises every day, boring through they were.

One of the many enjoyable things we did together was going to an old people's swimming class, mainly for those who had suffered strokes. It meant I could swim at my own pace and slowly get back into it. I'd originally learned to swim when I was seven so I thought I should be fine.

Ben learning to cycle again, on his dad's bike which is several sizes too big for him.

But I couldn't remember anything. I jumped happily off the side of the pool, but when I hit the water I couldn't swim anymore. I'd forget I had to kick my feet and paddle with my arms, and I just sank like a stone. I had to re-learn how to swim from the beginning, or what felt like the beginning. I started off learning to float and then moved towards breaststroke. Then I tried the front crawl, and it really felt like a wonderful sense of achievement when I got it.

The funny thing was, unbeknown to me, my arms didn't work in the same way as before. Instead of swimming in a straight line, I would swim in a roundabout motion or in big arcs. I quite often swam into the other people who were in the pool. Often, I would swim into these old ladies who would stop and sweetly apologise to me for the collision, but I'd get all pissed off and complain, *Why the hell has this woman swum into me!* I couldn't understand that I was the cause of these in-pool pile-ups. I was extremely lucky to have Andrew there to placate people on my behalf.

The fantastic thing about having Andrew was that he wasn't worried about doing things the way you were meant to. The NHS staff wanted to risk-assess everything first, whereas with Andrew – as long as we made things safe, like him running along next to the bike – whatever I wanted to try became possible. Most things didn't need a formal risk assessment; it was just a case of using common sense.

Tailoring my recovery process to me made it much more effective and become a reality, making me work as best as I could within what I knew and wanted to continue doing. It seems the formal institutions set up to help people recover from head traumas are very unadventurous with the care they offer to patients. For me, this didn't work, as I needed to take my recovery in whatever direction made the most sense to me. It was doing this that has made my recovery path very different from what you might expect after a serious head injury.

Within this flexible approach to my recovery, I became hell-bent on recovering as much of the old Ben as I could. I wanted to re-establish 'Ben' again – and there were no holds barred. The process involved trying to do things even if I wasn't ready for them. I didn't worry about not succeeding; it was the trying that mattered to me. Failure was a good learning process, not an end point.

Andrew, Ben's carer

I worked directly with Ben as his rehabilitation therapist, PA and carer for about eight months from February 2011. The first time I met him was at the interview for the position, in January. I remember Ben didn't speak much but his serene presence made up for that. While his parents did most of the talking, Ben sat calmly beside me, smiling through the entire 45 minutes or so while I was questioned about my CV and background. Later on, he told me he liked me the most out of the lot they had interviewed, which had been a funny mix of people. I liked him, too, from the start.

I had no idea what Ben was like before his accident. To me, he was just Ben – a quiet, relaxed and smiley fella, though that impression was soon to change as I got to know him. I wouldn't say it was difficult to work with him. At times it was challenging but it was always interesting and, most of the time, funny as hell. My experience with him taught me about patience and understanding and, most of all, how not to hit an old lady in the face while doing the backstroke.

Initially I spent five or six days a week working with Ben as part of a multidisciplinary team led by a certain clinical neuro-psychologist (aka 'The Devil'). My role was to aid Ben in his rehabilitation – specifically physically, mentally and socially – and to support his care from all disciplines as part of his recovery.

Even early on, I remember hearing a lot about the psychologist. Everyone spoke badly of her, especially Ben. Apparently she had made him feel uncomfortable and had insulted him.

I met her, and the entire team, for the first time at the initial meeting for Ben's rehab team. We all introduced ourselves, each person giving their thoughts on Ben and what we would do to help him. The physiotherapist spoke first, followed by the speech therapist, occupational therapists, clinical psychologists, social worker, his parents (both educational psychologists), then me – the medical school drop-out. The meeting went well and it seemed everyone was keen to do his or her utmost for Ben.

I recall Ben's mother taking me aside afterwards, as I put on my jacket in the hall. 'Ben used to be quite passive before,' she said, and continued to explain how he had always been that way in the past but had now changed and was more forthcoming. It was almost as though she was warning me about what I was up against. What she really meant was Ben had become explicitly blunt and devilishly outspoken.

Very quickly, I learned to understand how Ben's condition impacted on his life. I became aware of his sometimes unusual or inappropriate behaviour and comments, and his susceptibility to lethargy and mood swings. I realised Ben was very sensitive to physical and social activity and it affected him greatly, specifically his mood and emotional behaviour. The more he could participate in (without overdoing it), the more positive and alert he became. This became a very important part of his rehabilitation, so his family and I began to add more of these activities into his programme.

When Ben initially asked me to contribute to this book, in an email in April 2012, I replied saying I would be happy to. 'God knows what I will say,' I added. He answered, 'What about "Ben thinks everything is shit, especially the NHS. Oh, and Oxfam too."' Yes, that's Ben as I knew him when we first met.

Ben's favourite phrase for some time was, 'That is shit.' Generally, anything that was popular, different, weird or had some connection to his past that affected him in a way he was previously displeased with, was 'so shit'.

I appreciated his honesty. I wasn't about to judge his world, which at that point was viewed through the fragile and healing mind of a post-brain-injured guy. Mostly, I found it interesting and refreshing to hear his perspective on why lots of things were 'so shitty'.

We laughed a lot about these musings and I think it helped him deal with the frustrations and anger in a positive way. Later, he admitted he realised he did keep going on about certain topics, and I and other people should stop him from getting over-zealous about them. I thought this might have come from the fact some of his friends and family were now telling him they kept on hearing about Oxfam, the NHS, a particular doctor, the neuro-psychologist and Bono over and over again...

At the beginning, Ben's mood was often a bit slow and sleepy in the mornings, though by early afternoon he was raring to go. He got very tired very easily when I first started working with him and would usually have to take an afternoon nap, though this happened less often over time.

As I say, there were a few distinct topics that sent him off into a mild rage or rant. We joke and laugh about it now, as we did then. It never got in the way of our work or friendship. I found it more funny than offensive, as Ben and his parents filled me in on the reasons behind his disgust for certain things. It was good for him to get whatever was bothering him out, and the anger, we learned, was part of the recovery process. When the mind is healing, it easily becomes fatigued because of all the reformatting and reprocessing involved due to so many new neurological pathways forming and reforming. You can link this to the way a person is more likely to become cranky with little or no sleep. That was something Ben and his healing brain needed a lot of. Though perhaps cranky is the wrong word for Ben. He just knew what he liked and didn't like.

From the outset we attended a swimming class at the local pool twice a week. Hugh and Jenny suggested it would be a good idea and I agreed, as did the team physiotherapist, Dulcie. Initially she joined us at the pool and together we developed an exercise plan to follow. Ben had been a strong swimmer before his accident but now he could barely remain afloat for longer than a few seconds, if at all. We needed to build up his muscle strength after the excessive muscle wastage from being confined to bed for so long, and develop his arm and leg co-ordination so he wasn't flapping about in the water like a baby at bath time. Ben also needed to re-learn the different swimming strokes, which he seemed to vaguely remember but couldn't quite execute correctly.

So every Tuesday and Thursday morning, from 9 to 11, we attended the class along with a large group of elderly men and women. We soon found out the group was quite taken with these two young lads. Everyone wanted to know Ben's story and we happily answered all their questions. The other thing that made us stand out from the crowd was that we didn't follow the class, instead following our own routines and practising the exercises Dulcie had taught us.

After a month or so, Ben was managing quite well with the aid of floats. Dulcie was amazed at the progress. But we didn't stop there. Within another couple of months, he was doing the backstroke and front crawl completely on his own, without needing to stop every so often. Dulcie wasn't the only one who was impressed: the entire swimming class had witnessed Ben's transformation and was elated, too.

One thing Ben did have a lot of trouble with at the pool was inserting the pound coin into the locker. He still had difficulty controlling the head shakes he suffered from, which in turn caused his hands to tremor, losing a good deal of hand co-ordination as a result. Every day we would work on hand exercises, practising them for up to an hour. Eventually Ben's shaking and hand tremors mellowed and his co-ordination improved greatly, thanks to his dedication with the hand exercises and swimming. By the time we left the swimming classes, he was able to insert the pound coin himself.

The whole process of going to the pool, getting changed and so on was a complete, holistic exercise, good for Ben in so many ways, not just physically but also for his social and mental rehabilitation. Initially, I would accompany him to the pool from his home, share a cubicle to help him get changed, secure him a locker and see he got into the water safely. After a short while, the physiotherapist and I, together with his parents, decided Ben should start doing some of these things on his own. So, instead of meeting him at his house, I met him at the pool. Then Ben started using his own cubicle and changing by himself.

Some time later, in the car on our way home from the pool, Ben told me – and his slightly embarrassed dad – he thought I'd left him to get changed on his own because he'd once asked me, 'So, are you gay?', while we were changing in the cubicle together, and I hadn't answered. To the best of my recollection, this never happened. At least, I never heard him ask the question. Confabulation or not, it was one of those funny moments when neither his dad nor I knew quite what to say. Looking back now, I guess Ben was perhaps letting me know that he knew I was gay and he was okay with it. We had always spent most of our conversations talking about his life, past and present, his rehabilitation and his relationship with Jazz. After that day,

I spoke more openly with Ben about my own life, as he was quite interested to get to know me, and later I introduced him to my partner, Guillermo.

We were well-liked by the people in the swimming class, especially the ladies, and they openly welcomed our attendance at every session – so much so, they would ask where we'd been if we happened to miss a day. Of course, Ben would later inform his parents, 'The old ladies were chatting up Andrew again at the pool today.'

The swimming proved a very positive experience for Ben. He had become more independent and confident in his daily tasks. He also loved to interact with different people at the pool and have fun while he was there. Much to the total shock and, dare I say, horror, of the rehabilitation team, we liked to make use of the indoor slide after all his exercises were done and lengths completed. Ben – or maybe it was both of us – was so enthusiastic about the slide we would even ask the pool attendants to open it if it was closed, so we could use it. We laughed a lot and, like two little boys, our time at the pool was not complete unless we got to go on the slide.

After almost four months of attending the classes, Ben and I decided it was time for a change. The exercises and short lengths were no longer useful and he was now ready to swim full lengths in proper swimming lanes during public hours, away from the comfort and security of a class or group. So we switched to a different pool and began another, more intensive, swimming routine, much to the dismay of the abandoned old ladies.

The routine I set up for Ben for the lane-swimming sessions involved ten lengths of breaststroke, ten lengths of backstroke and ten of front crawl. At this stage I had also started teaching swimming classes to children at weekends and had a better idea of what Ben should be doing to perfect his strokes. Initially, he could only manage five or six full lengths of each style, but after some time he was doing the full thirty lengths along with me, and doing an excellent job at that.

Once, during one of our swimming sessions, Ben was doing backstroke in an area that was not a designated swimming lane (sometimes he preferred this, if there were too many people in one lane). He could now swim well but his spatial awareness was still a bit off and as he reached the other end of the pool he crashed with an elderly man. He was sure it was the elderly man who had crashed into him, and he wasn't letting it go. This time, unlike the occasions at the old people's class, he proceeded to get very angry with the man and, from what I could tell from across the pool, cursed the poor fella right out of it. Of course, the man soon realised it was a big misunderstanding, but Ben didn't, and swam off in a huff.

A few minutes later he was divulging all to me in an angry rant in the showers.

'How could he not know I was swimming? What a prick!' he said, still mystified.

'Well, Ben, you were swimming in a kind of diagonal. How could you not bump into someone?' I told him, and we laughed.

On the days we didn't go to the pool, we would walk to the park instead and continue with some exercises there using the public exercise contraptions, which Ben enjoyed more than I did. Chatting one day over breakfast with his parents, we decided it would be good to try to get him riding a bike again and, after the success with the swimming, we thought, *why not?*

'I don't think it's a good idea,' said a member of the rehabilitation team. We'd been getting a lot of that lately. Ben believed we didn't need to get anyone's permission or convince anyone what we were doing was right. If he wanted to do something, and I was there supporting him, then he would do it and it would be okay. So we borrowed Hugh's bike and helmet, and off we went to the park. 'It's not as if we're going cycling along the M4,' Ben said. In fact, the park was an ideal place to practise as it had plenty of open space and, of course, the added safety of grass. Initially, we couldn't stop laughing as Ben kept toppling over. He never hurt himself and was safely falling beside me on the soft ground. So he could get in a good cycle around the park, we would go to the top of a small hill in the centre to help him gather a bit of speed. Ben would balance himself by sitting on the seat of the bike with one foot on a pedal and one foot on the ground. At first I would hold the back of the bike as he cycled along the grass, but eventually he managed to balance and ride the bike alone.

At the beginning of June, my other work commitments meant I could work with Ben only three or four days a week. This was good for him, as it forced him to be less reliant on my assistance and gave him the opportunity to become even more independent. Plus, he had planned on attending a gym and going to Tai Chi classes in his increasing free time. My work was almost done.

I worked very closely with Ben so I built a strong bond with him and a high level of trust, which allowed me to be actively involved in all aspects of his care. This was important, as I was the only one from the rehab team who saw him daily. We communicated a lot, which was very important for him, as rehabilitation is as much about actually feeling better in yourself, and understanding and processing what is happening to you, your body and your mind, as it is about getting 'better' and fitter in every way.

I learned from my time with Ben that often what someone is really dealing with may be very far removed from what you imagine, and that a sense of humour (and plenty of cups of tea) will get you through anything.

Jenny

When Andrew asked the physio about taking Ben swimming, she suggested the Dolphin Swimming Club. This was a morning class at a local pool for those recovering from accidents or strokes who would better cope with a quieter time not open to public swimming. The regulars were mainly – though not exclusively – older people recovering from strokes.

The weekly sessions were a social event for Dolphin members and the swimming was usually followed by coffee. For weeks, Andrew was asked whether they could stay for a coffee; for weeks, Andrew declined with the excuse of getting back for an appointment. However, one week towards the end of their Dolphin sessions, Andrew failed to resist the ever-more pressing invitation. I was later regaled with an amusing tale of Ben's displeasure with Andrew's acceptance, with Ben vowing he would never have gone for a coffee with 'old' people after swimming before his accident, so why should it be okay to do so now? A little disappointed at his lack of generosity, I pointed out how they'd celebrated his progress and obviously saw him as one of theirs. This set him off again, supported by the customary directness and use of colourful language! This was their only coffee with the rest of the Dolphins.

Ben's breathing was still very noisy as a result of his tracheotomy, and it could be alarming to anyone who didn't know him. When he started to go to the pool on his own, this disturbed the lifeguards, who watched him anxiously and would approach him to see if he was okay. Other swimmers asked whether he was asthmatic. At first Ben explained it was the tracheotomy, and sometimes further questions would result in him telling his story to people who probably wished they hadn't asked. Once, according to Ben, his story left some poor, well-meaning lady clinging to the side of the pool in a state of shock. He decided it might be better to say it was the result of throat surgery from then on. We agreed it might also be a good idea to warn the lifeguard.

Many swimming towels were lost at the pool and others brought home that didn't belong to us. Goggles were also left behind, along with swimming trunks and various other items of clothing. The habit of leaving, mislaying or losing things remains – but this was a bit of a trait even before the accident. I soon organised the towels so he took those on top of the pile – the ones he'd acquired from previous swimming sessions. Funnily enough, he didn't seem to lose these. We also learned to buy cheaper items of clothing, such as coats and jackets, so as not to fret about things lost.

As a family, we often swim in the sea off the south coast, and three years on from Ben coming home, we're in the sea for a summer's swim once again. I hear the regular splash of someone swimming behind me and turn to see Ben confidently powering away, doing an impressive front crawl with no hint of any physical weakness. He had always been a confident swimmer. He will now go down to the beach for a swim even if we're not with him.

Ben

Angie is a voice coach who works with people who have to speak in public. As an acquaintance of my parents, she'd heard about what had happened and offered to undertake some voice work with me.

By May, the support from the neuro-rehabilitation team had finished and I was left to my own devices. Angie helped me grow in confidence with my voice. She got me to do all kinds of exercises, including lots of voice modulation – close to singing – to exercise my voice by working at different pitches. This proved a really good way to improve my voice control.

The support Angie gave me was fantastically helpful and enabled me to strengthen my voice as best I could. Although she did all these voice-strengthening exercises with me, I think the thing she really helped me with most was practising how to introduce myself at university. I was making plans to go back to do another master's degree later in the year, and I wanted to be able to introduce myself to the other students in a way that wouldn't totally freak people out and scare them off. Angie also went through how I would explain to people what had happened to me. These run-throughs made a good way to direct the help Angie could give me, although she also had to put up with my rather rude language, which was still pretty extreme at this stage of my recovery.

Angie, Ben's voice coach

'So I guess we'd better say how awful the news is about Ben, eh?' This was the first I'd heard about Ben's accident. We were at a friend's house for dinner and they'd found out about it from someone else who'd heard from another person – and so the Chinese whispers had continued. In fact, among Hugh and Jenny's wide circle of friends, I'd say we were about the last to know. There weren't adequate words to express what we felt and thought that evening and they were a very strange few hours. All we could do was send messages of support (thank goodness for text and email) so the family knew we were thinking about them. Did we all privately think, *How on earth are they going to get through this?* Probably. Did we all suddenly want to talk to our own children? Desperately. Did we all feel utterly useless and helpless? Most definitely.

It seems a long time since those conversations and, although I kept in touch with Jenny via text, it wasn't until Christmas 2010 that we spoke at length. That was when Hugh and Jenny asked me if I might do some voice work with Ben when he was strong enough and, of course, I said yes.

In March 2011, the choir I sing with did a concert. Hugh and Jenny brought Ben along and that was the first time he saw me, although I didn't see him. When we met a week later, I asked him what he'd thought of the evening. He was honest enough to say he was glad he'd come along but thought the music was pretty boring. And that was the foundation of what became an honest and open way of working together.

For my part, I said from the start I wasn't sure I could make a difference. Ben, however, was up for anything, and was so determined he went for my crazy vocal exercises with more effort than I could have imagined possible. Good job they live in a big house with thick walls!

Physically, at that time Ben was quite wobbly on his legs and tired easily. He sounded hesitant and his voice was husky and strained. But there was also energy there and such a twinkle in his eyes that I was hopeful. I've worked with people whose eyes have 'given up' somehow and they don't have the will to communicate. With Ben,

I knew straight away he had lots to say and that he wanted to make connections with people again.

We began with breathing, the foundation for everything that happens vocally. Quite simply, without breath there is no voice. We breathed and breathed together. Gradually, we added vocal sounds. I always left him a sheet of notes so he could practise in between our sessions. I also suggested we did some upper body exercises to loosen up. We swung our arms, opened our chests, rolled our shoulders and then fell about laughing. We worked for about 40 minutes at a time and then talked about everything else – films, TV, friends, exercise and, of course, any memories Ben had of 'before'.

One aspect I wanted to tackle, when I heard Ben was planning to go back to university, was his choice of language. I wasn't sure how to broach this, but then remembered the only way to approach anything with him was to get on with it and just be totally straightforward.

So I said, 'Ben, when you meet your seminar group for the first time, I'd suggest you don't use the word "fuck".'

He looked a bit surprised and asked me why.

I said, 'Well, there may be people there who have strong feelings about language and you wouldn't want to offend them. Also, there may be people from other countries who don't even know what it means – do you really want to have to explain that?'

He grinned and I think that was a bit of a landmark because it was a joke between us and Ben totally 'got it'.

Don't think for one minute Ben was always cheerful and in a great mood. He had a lot of anger and at times he seemed terribly fed up. I also thought there was a danger of him becoming bored with life. I wonder what was going on inside his mind during those early months.

Sometimes I came away from seeing him feeling we'd made huge progress, and sometimes I wasn't sure. It was only when I saw him after a break of a couple of months that it became clear how much he had developed since our first meeting.

Ben

As my home rehab was winding down, I decided to go to a gym on the recommendation of my parents. They went there and knew the trainers. They decided to ask a trainer called Alex whether he would mind getting me fit again.

I'd never been a fan of the gym. I used to get my exercise by rock climbing, running and using my bike as a means of getting around, so the gym was very alien to me. I always imagined them full of body-builders rather than fit, healthy individuals.

At the time, though, I really needed to improve my fitness. We discussed the gym with one of the physiotherapists on my rehab team. She was fairly sceptical but agreed to meet the trainer to make sure he knew what to work on and to satisfy herself he would do me no harm.

We had this meeting at the gym, where Alex sat down with me, my mum and the physiotherapist. It was an odd meeting. The phys-iotherapist kept telling Alex he had to help strengthen this muscle or that muscle. She was using technical terms for each muscle, which I didn't understand, and I think it scared him off rather than encour-aged him to work with me.

The one thing it did do, though, was formalise our relationship and show he was entering into a serious enterprise. My gym sessions were fairly formal and exceptionally hard work to start with. Although I'm sure Alex gave me exercises that were breaking me in gently, they were still exhausting and generally I would leave the place dripping with sweat. Other people in the gym would say to Alex, 'What are you doing to him?' My breathing was heavier than it used to be, as a result of the tracheotomy. This meant he often had to reassure people it was nothing to worry about and I wasn't about to peg out.

Alex and I worked well together. He knew what was too much for me but also knew I would try my best to complete whatever chal-lenge he set. So we developed a relationship where I would do what-ever he wanted me to. It would physically exhaust me but I knew it was good for me. It's absurd that I needed to get run over in order to realise hating the gym was simply a matter of habit.

Alex, Ben's personal trainer

My first session with Ben was in June 2011. It was unlike any other personal training session I'd ever done. I'd worked with people with injuries before, but this was something big.

I'd known Ben's parents for a few years, as they'd been members at the gym I worked in. One day, Jenny approached and told me about Ben's accident and what condition he was now in, and asked if I'd work with him. I agreed and we arranged a meeting with Ben and his physiotherapist. During the meeting, I got a whistle-stop tour of the past eight months of Ben's life: the accident, his recovery and the physiotherapy he'd been going through.

For our first few sessions, Ben was very quiet, hardly saying a word. I took this to be part shyness and part being slightly overwhelmed by the whole situation – being in a gym, trying to re-build your life and body after almost dying a few months earlier. At that time, he also seemed almost a little uneasy in his own body, probably for the same reason.

After a few weeks, however, Ben started coming out of his shell. We were combining general strength work with co-ordination and functional movements, and he was making slow but steady progress. I'll never forget the first time Ben swore at me. He was on his third set of press-ups and coming to the end of the agreed repetitions. He clearly had a few more in the tank, so I said, 'That was too easy – three more, please.' At which he looked up, sweat dripping off his nose and, through a wheezing throat, simply croaked, 'Bastard!', then proceeded to do as he was asked.

One of my philosophies of training is that movement is important. 'Train movements, not muscles' is the catchphrase in the industry. This has been the way I've worked with Ben from the very start. Rather than having a specific injury or weakness, which would require a certain muscle to be rehabilitated, his needs involved re-learning how to do almost everything he physically used to be able to do. We started with the absolute basics: pushing objects overhead; stepping forward and backward; rotating. The things people take for granted in everyday life.

Over the first 18 months of working with Ben, my understanding of his injuries became clearer. All these movements we were working on, they were all inside his brain somewhere. They needed to be found and re-awoken. 'Dusting them off' is the term I've often used with him.

As well as motor difficulties, Ben's breathing was a bit of an issue for a few months. When he was working hard, he would get a pretty serious wheeze on. When you're training someone and it sounds like they're having an asthma attack, it can be slightly disconcerting. Without wanting to ask too many questions about the accident, I remembered Ben was still seeing a speech therapist about his breathing, so we had a chat and he explained about the tracheotomy. We worked around the scary breathing for a while but, as his fitness improved, the workouts increased in intensity and he needed to warm up more. As any athlete will tell you, the better the warm-up, the easier the workout. Ben's warm-up routines were getting more intense, during which he was breathing hard, making quite a racket. However, after this initial tough ten minutes, his breathing was much easier for the rest of the session. We've kept the hard warm-ups and they still have the desired effect, as well as scaring the other people on the machines around the gym. They think I'm killing him!

Throughout my working relationship with Ben, I've never given him any special treatment based on his injuries. That would've been pointless, as my job was to get him back to where he was beforehand. I also never ask anything of him I don't think he can do, though whether he believes it or not at the start is a different story. It's the same with any other client – if they look at an exercise and say *I can't do that* but, as a trainer, I know they can, I don't pander to their apprehension. They've just got to get on with it.

The people who know Ben well know the condition he was in when we started working together. For those who don't, I can give you an example. Stand up straight. Step forward with your left leg. Now bring it back to where it started. Repeat with your right leg. This was the kind of thing Ben and I were working on when we first began training together.

Now, Ben does chin-ups. He can pick up the equivalent of his bodyweight off the floor. He does press-ups like they're child's play. The other week, I put a step platform in front of him and asked him to face away from the step, then jump onto it while spinning around 180 degrees in the air. Two things happened which show just how far he has come. Firstly, he said, 'Move over then,' so he could get on with it, without a moment's hesitation. Secondly, he nailed it.

I'd say Ben's confidence in himself and in his body's abilities is back. Plus, his motor skills, strength and co-ordination are one hundred times the level they were at when we began.

Ben

During my recuperation my father had been telling his friend Jim how I was still physically unsteady and wasn't very good at connecting my movements together. In response, Jim said he was doing Tai Chi and it might help. So Dad got Jim to speak to his teacher, Ali, about my situation and ask whether he thought Tai Chi would be a good idea. Ali said he expected it would, as it is a movement-focused meditation. He came over to my house one weekend to introduce me to some Tai Chi moves. This really showed how unsteady I was on my feet as I kept falling over in the positions I had to adopt.

I decided to give it a go, and to start with we did a lot of the practice sessions privately, indoors at home, which was best for me while I was so incredibly unstable. He got me used to the basic movements but I remained so precarious he agreed I shouldn't join his classes for a while. When it was warmer, we moved to doing sessions in the garden. He tried to encourage my mum to do the sessions with us, but that didn't last long. We continued these private sessions for the rest of the year, before he suggested I should join in with the classes he did locally.

Joining a group was a good move, as it also got me to socialise with local people and integrate more. Going to the Tai Chi classes has become a routine, which I am grateful for, and has served me well. It has helped to be surrounded by a number of people who have seen me over a few years and know what trials I have been through. They are mostly impressed by the fact I am now able to do the moves without falling over! I am generally more balanced than I was when I started and would certainly say Tai Chi has helped me.

Ali, Ben's Tai Chi teacher

One sunny Sunday afternoon in October 2011, about one year after Ben had his horrific accident, I stood outside the front door to his family home. I took a deep breath, gathered myself, and knocked. I had come to share my Tai Chi with him, hoping its magic would prove an effective cure for some of the problems I'd heard he was suffering from.

Ben was expecting me and answered the door himself. It was a tall, wide and rather solid door, and he appeared to be clinging onto it to keep himself from falling. He clumsily stepped back to open it wider and allow me in. When he let go of the door, I immediately sensed he was not a stable unit and primed myself to catch him as he extended his hand towards mine to shake hello.

Standing, Ben cut an odd figure. He is tall and well-built, but at that moment he was anything but strong. His head leaned over at an unnatural angle and he agitated uncontrollably, reminding me of a cow with BSE (Bovine Spongiform Encephalopathy, or Mad Cow Disease) or a Parkinsonian old gent. When walking, he was like a seriously off-kilter robot: stiff, tottering and clunky, his every step an improbable victory over gravity.

We went through to the kitchen and Ben's mum offered us a cup of tea before we started our session. It sounded like a good idea, a chance for the three of us to sit down and discuss the plan. I could find out about Ben and what he could or couldn't do, and he could hear a bit about Tai Chi from me. Like many people, he didn't really know much about it, but a friend had recommended me to the family and, importantly, he wanted to try it.

As we sat chatting, Ben would regularly gasp for breath, a sudden and noisy in-breath much like the noise you might make the moment you realise you've forgotten something really important. In Ben's case the thing he kept forgetting was the small matter of breathing in.

Ben sat sloped diagonally across a kitchen chair, draping himself over the edge, the backrest of the chair tucked under one of his armpits. Was it due to his accident he couldn't sit straight? Or was it down to his irreverent attitude to life that he sat like this? Either way, I could see the scale of his problems. Some vital internal functioning had taken a real hit and his balance and motor control weren't right.

We talked about the accident and his process of recovery to date. Ben said he was only now able to consider doing something like Tai Chi. For the past year he had been concentrating on the real basics: being able to get out of bed, learning to walk and swim again. It had already been an arduous process of re-learning things he had previously taken for granted.

Of course it wasn't just physically that Ben had been severely damaged. A look through the opening to the dining area gave a clue to the psychological side to his recovery. Along the wall was a length of paper, perhaps four or five metres long. A timeline had been drawn, starting from his birth on the left and progressing right up to the date of his accident on the right. Along this timeline were hand-written notes of stages and events, such as school, university, holidays, travel, houses he'd lived in and photos of people he knew. By this stage, a year after his accident, Ben had recovered many memories of his life before. But he couldn't remember Jazz, his girlfriend who died so tragically, and he couldn't remember the accident either.

Talking about this, I felt a real weight hit my stomach. I wondered if perhaps these memories might all come flooding back as we started working Ben's body back to better functioning, as if these memories might be stored in the knots and twists of the muscles and tendons rather than in Ben's full consciousness. It had already taken a huge amount of time and effort to get to this point, where he would be able to attempt most Tai Chi exercises. But the process of continuing this Herculean effort of getting back to a more natural state would require improvement on many levels, and I was fearful that, to progress, he might have to re-live some of the horrors he had been through.

Having heard all about Ben, it was my turn to give him an introduction to the world of Tai Chi and explain how it might help him. Tai Chi is called an internal martial art, to distinguish it from external martial arts such as karate or boxing. The latter emphasise muscularity, cardio-vascular fitness, speed and raw strength. Tai Chi has a different way of working, which stems from its emergence from a culture of Chinese philosophy and Chinese medicine.

The Tai Chi way of exercising is a world away from jogging while plugged into music or pumping iron in a gym with a sound-system blaring. These modern kinds of exercise are simply a way of keeping the body in shape. The mind is viewed as totally unimportant and uninvolved in this process, to the point where it needs to be kept entertained while the body does its thing. In Tai Chi, by contrast, you must pay extremely close and careful attention to what is going on in the body. In fact, the mind plays the primary role in each and every operation.

So as I sat there at Ben's breakfast table, explaining how Tai Chi works, I hoped we would be able to restore his body to its natural state rather than the stressed-out one it was currently in. Although his body was, at this stage, a mess (to put it mildly), it is true to say almost everyone's body would benefit from a return to more natural usage. So Ben started in exactly the same way all my students do, with a set of introductory exercises called Fan Song Gong, designed to loosen up the body and the joints in order to get them ready to work together as a whole.

That first day, Ben struggled with almost everything in our run-through of the 18 movements of Fan Song Gong. Normally, one hour of a three-hour one-to-one class would suffice for this set but most of these basic movements were a struggle and we would often have to find ways to make them possible, such as by Ben leaning on furniture, or on me. We carefully focused on each of the fundamental exercises, working our way through all the main joints of the body, gradually opening them up again and encouraging natural circular, twining movements to come back into Ben's body.

For the next stage, we moved from the kitchen into the front study. In Tai Chi philosophy there is a saying, 'Close all the doors.' This is the practice of shutting off external stimulation and focusing your attention inside, to become aware of what is happening in the body. In this quiet space I introduced Ben to the Tai Chi practice that comes from the ancient Dao Yin exercise method, which carefully guides the movements of the body with the use of the mind. This exercise is both extremely simple and extremely profound.

We stood facing each other, feet shoulder-width apart, very still and motionless. I wanted Ben to relax, not just a bit, but deeply. The beginning of this exercise is like the moment you hit the pillow after a long day. You are finally able to let go of the stresses and strains of the day. You exhale and your whole body sinks into the comfort of your bed. That is the approach to this exercise: we must relax, and it must feel like a release.

I asked him to bring his attention to his breathing. He was still gasping at odd intervals. I said, 'Just concentrate on your breath now, Ben. When you breathe in, where does it go? How are you breathing? Is it quick? Is it shallow? Let's make it smooth. Nice and smooth and deep. Don't hold your breath in the lungs; let it drop down deeper than that. Expand it as you breathe in, contract it as you breathe out. Feel yourself expand and contract, expand and contract.'

Over the weeks, I never really knew if Ben was fully into the exercises. He worked hard in our sessions but he didn't always do his 'homework'. To begin with, he had not only major balance problems but also trouble remembering the movements. His execution of them was very stiff at first, but became softer over time. In general, his progress was much more visible over a long period rather than from week to week but he is now straighter, doesn't twitch, doesn't gasp for breath and is quite steady and stable.

Ben

After a few weeks of working at home with Ali, he suggested I join the regular group sessions he organises in Brighton. Tai Chi remains a regular commitment and I make sure that my twice-weekly sessions fit into my life. I'm grateful to Ali for sticking with me, for his patience and for his inclusive teaching that still takes into account my poor memory and wonky balance. The group has also been so tolerant of me. I'm sure that my movements haven't always contributed to the flow of the session! It's one of the new things since my accident that has allowed me to enjoy belonging to a group, and to one that would probably never have figured in my life if Ali hadn't been willing to take me on as a bit of a challenge! Tai Chi has been a very positive thing for me to stick to as it focuses on the quality of my movements and has a very different aim from going to the gym, making them ideal activities to do in tandem.

In February 2012, I ran the Brighton Half Marathon. I put my name down and then, when I told two of my friends, Morgan and Roland, they decided to do it as well. It became a three-way pact.

At the time, Morgan was studying to become a doctor at Brighton University so he was around enough to be able to train with me and we started just after Christmas. Training was essential to make sure we were up to the rigours of running that distance. In many ways it was about pushing myself to the limit, to prove to myself and others I could still do that.

I used to train for marathons before the accident. In fact, I was supposed to run a marathon in Brighton in April 2010, a few months before the accident. In the end I couldn't do it as I was in Berlin and couldn't fly back because of an ash cloud caused by a volcano in Iceland. Planes across Europe were grounded, and so was I.

This time, I didn't want to miss my chance. I'd already started going on runs in the park with my dad so to begin with I got fit by myself, continuing and increasing these runs. I discovered I was still breathing extremely heavily. It was so bad, dogs in the park would get agitated and bark at me furiously as I ran past them. A group of children walking home from school would take the piss out of me and mimic my breathing, annoying me intensely. However, it did seem that now, when I was breathing noisily, it was mainly just when I was very out of breath. I was literally gasping for breath.

Morgan had also been doing initial training so we met up for longer runs, which meant we couldn't stick to the park. Instead we ran along the beach, which would form much of the route of the half-marathon itself.

With the training I had done, I quite easily ran up to ten miles with Morgan and felt comfortable with that distance. I hadn't run with Roland but he said he'd also run ten miles and was fairly confident with that too. So we were all certain we could manage the distance without any problems.

On the day of the event, in mid-February, we met up on the seafront, where the half-marathon was due to start. It was a crisp, sunny morning, which was perfect weather for the event – not too cold and not wet. Morgan had printed us all team T-shirts, which were orange and had our team name printed on the front. We were called Team Abasanjo. All our parents were there to support us.

The start was packed with hundreds of people getting in place for the off. At this point we were busy just making sure we didn't lose each other in the crowd. As the race started, we continued to keep an eye on each other so we wouldn't get separated. Everything seemed fine and we were going strongly for the first stretch. We seemed to be making good time and were about mid-pack.

About halfway along I was desperate for some water but I hadn't brought any. I asked Morgan and Roland, but they hadn't either, so I had to carry on desperately thirsty. Another runner, a lady close by, heard me asking and gave me some of hers. As we carried on, there were drink stations with plenty of free water, which I was very grateful for.

There was also a point when my breathing became very heavy; I think it was as I became more and more tired. Another lady started saying to me, 'Are you all right?' I was wheezing so much I couldn't properly respond without stopping, which I didn't want to do. Thankfully, Morgan realised I couldn't answer and said, 'Ben breathes very heavily. That's just the way he is.' I'm glad he didn't say any more about what had happened to me; it's not something you really need to go into part-way round a half-marathon.

It was all going fine until we got to the ten-mile mark, where we'd run as far as we could along the seafront and were meant to turn back. At this point the tiredness overtook me. I was totally exhausted. I told Roland and Morgan I didn't think I could keep going. They were also at the limit of their endurance, having only trained up to ten miles as well. Even though we were getting very near the end, with just three miles to go, we had all hit a wall.

I just couldn't face it. I stopped and wouldn't run anymore. Morgan and Roland stopped with me as I struggled to find the courage to go further. There we were, standing at the end of the promenade, watching hundreds of people go past. We must have waited for five minutes or more to recover, with most of the runners overtaking us. We knew we had only three more miles to do, along the seafront route Morgan and I had trained on. It was only after the crowds began to ease that I felt I'd recovered enough to do the last little stretch, and finish. We decided to dig deep and run those last few miles. I thought I'd got just enough energy in reserve to do it.

From that moment on, I got a second wind, knowing how close I was to finishing, and it seemed more manageable. Both Roland and

Morgan also seemed to get into their stride. We got a big cheer when we went past my family, who were looking out for us as we were coming up to the finish.

Brighton Half Marathon "with a little help from my friends" – Ben, Roland and Morgan, February 2012

In the end, we completed the half-marathon in about two hours and fifteen minutes – a relatively slow but still respectable time. Crossing the line, I mostly felt relief that I had done it, and that I could stop pushing my body any further as it had just about reached its limit. Having trained a distance of ten miles, I did these comfortably, but the last three miles I had to do to complete the full half-marathon were where it really hurt. But I also felt a sense of accomplishment. After all I had been through, it was fantastic that I had the capabilities to run a half-marathon – undeterred by barking dogs and piss-taking kids!

Finding Myself

I remember thinking that if his sense of humour was intact, then the damage to his brain couldn't have been too severe.
Gideon Susman, a friend since childhood, on first visiting Ben in hospital

*

Ben

Having been under the constraints of the NHS neuro-rehabilitation programme to get physically back into shape, finally being signed-off it meant a chance to enjoy the summer. I wanted to get back to real life and reaffirm many of my old habits before undertaking another form of exercise by going back to university to regain my intellectual abilities.

This was a time when I was rediscovering all the things I used to like and do, and reclaiming my love of music and fun. These were areas I needed to explore for my own peace of mind.

So, who was I?

Initially, I learned from 'the wall' and everyone around me who could explain how the parts of my life fitted together when I could not. Then memories started to come back – a process that was joyous when I could remember parts of my life I hadn't been able to before. From what I have remembered as time has gone on, here is how I would summarise my life before the accident.

I was brought up in Brighton and Hove on the south coast of England, where the white cliffs fall into the Channel and draw your gaze to the horizon. And my horizon was wide. The eldest of three children – my sister and brother are two and six years younger than me, respectively – I was always the adventurous one and, of course, the first to do most things.

My mum is half French and so the idea of living abroad was familiar to me. After finishing my A-levels, the obvious first stop was France, where I spent my days in the sunshine, picking grapes in a vineyard and picking up more than a just smattering of French. Although my mother is fluent, she hadn't spoken it to us as children so it was good to properly get to grips with the language.

I also set off further afield, visiting a friend who was working with Tibetan monks in India, teaching them English and general knowledge. I then travelled to Peru to work with a charity providing education to children who were disabled.

This call to adventure and travel was not quenched that year. As an undergraduate student at Bath University, where I studied economics and international development, I had the opportunity to spend a year as a researcher on a wellbeing project in Thailand. Working on this project, I was able to talk to a lot of people about their needs and drives, to construct a research model of wellbeing and how people conceptualise it. After that, my mind was set: I would work on projects to help people in developing countries, which would give me the chance both to help others and to travel and see the world.

But things are not always so easy. After graduating in 2006, I had to work in bars and restaurants just to keep my head above water and it was only in 2007 that I eventually found work at a Brighton-based development consultancy. I was in charge of putting together the company's bids to secure them work over the next few months. This experience gave me an insight into what makes people attractive to funding organisations and donors alike. After a year-and-a-half I realised if I wanted to really 'do development' I would need a master's degree and I enrolled on the development management course at the London School of Economics (LSE).

London is an expensive city, and rather than throw money down the drain on rent – which I couldn't afford anyway – my parents bought me a narrowboat to live on during the course and then hopefully sell on without a loss. So I lived on the canals of North London for a year.

In winter this was a bit of a nightmare. I particularly remember that the winter after I'd got the boat was freezing. To heat the place, I had to be able to start a fire, which meant I had to stock up enough coal. Sometimes I got iced in, it was so cold. Then in summer I had to keep moving every two weeks to avoid having to pay for a mooring. But living on the boat was a great experience. It was easily the cheapest way to live in London and the only way I could afford to enjoy such a bohemian life when I didn't have an income. In summer, especially, it was a glorious way to spend my days and a great place for friends to congregate.

While on the master's course, I made a number of good friends who I am still in touch with, and it was during this year of boating, studying, relaxing and partying that I met Jazz. We got together through doing the same course at LSE. Everyone tells me her relaxed approach to life was very similar to mine.

My life on the boat gave me the opportunity to think through my dreams and work out how to take my life in my chosen direction, and after my year at LSE things began to fall into place. The course had given me experience of managing development projects, which was what I needed to be able to work in this field effectively. I worked for Oxfam in Kenya, did an internship with Transparency International in Berlin and was accepted onto an Overseas Development Institute

Ben on his narrowboat, stopping for the night on the Thames at Windsor after finishing his master's at LSE, Summer 2009

(ODI) fellowship programme to work as an economist for the Rwandan government for two years.

After a few hiccups, Jazz found work with a non-governmental organisation (and later with the UN) in Haiti, and we made long-term plans for her to move to Rwanda when her contract was up so we could live together and look towards the future.

Of course, that was never to be. And, just for a while, the laid-back, positive, active person I was also sank with little trace.

When I think about my experience, I see I have demonstrated resilience and vulnerability at the same time. My body survived without a broken bone and my brain injury has continued to heal, despite scans that suggested I had suffered disruption at a cellular level. However, recovering from such an injury saw other vulnerabilities occur.

For a while, I had a lower tolerance for alcohol. Drinking has always been an important part of my social life, and my body's inability to cope with alcohol meant I got drunk easily, sometimes completely forgetting what had happened and how I'd got home after the pub. This made my parents very anxious. I felt my mum, in particular, wanted to wrap me up in cotton-wool and protect me from what used to be a normal part of my life.

My friends were also concerned and were constantly monitoring my alcohol intake. For a while I was teetotal because I couldn't handle it as I used to. I realised how boring drunk people are to hang around with when you can't drink; there are only so many times you can handle hearing the same story again and again.

My accident has also made me vulnerable in my relationships with others. Since the accident, some people have behaved differently towards me. I feel some even used my experience for their own ends. After I came out of hospital, I found out a friend of mine had published a blog about his interaction with me, which I saw as a total invasion of my privacy. I still don't know why he did it. Perhaps it was his way of coping with the accident but he went ahead without considering whether I would want it talked about in that way, something I very much resent.

For Jazz's family, particularly her mum, Abby, I became the primary link to Jazz and to her life before the accident. I had known Jazz's family before my memory loss as I'd been to Montréal with Jazz to visit her family and friends, who lived there.

At that point, soon after the accident, Abby was in regular email contact with my mum and had been very supportive to my parents. After I left hospital she would phone up regularly to speak to them and then to me. I was very quiet at that time and not very comprehensible. After a while my speech got better, to the point where I could have a chat with her about what I was doing and give weekly updates on how my rehab was going. For a time, Abby's calls became part of my routine, something fitted in among the general assortment of carer visits and rehab activities.

Later on, Abby and Jazz's sister, Kiran, came over on separate occasions to see relatives in the UK and took the opportunity to visit me and see how I was doing. I recognised Abby but not Kiran, although I'd also met her in Montréal. Andrew and I took them to our favourite Thai restaurant for a meal. I felt that meeting them both was good; to see the connection they felt between us, even if it was lost on me.

Abby continued to phone up every week to see how I was getting on. This was part of my normal routine and only became problematic when it became obvious she was blaming the accident on drunk drivers. My dad told me that the police hadn't had breathalysers but the officers arresting the two drivers involved had said they hadn't seemed drunk when they picked them up shortly after the accident. So I told Abby this didn't seem to be the case. I said, 'Come on, it was terrible but you can't be blaming this calamity on other things. You need to accept it was an accident.' I really felt very strongly that there wasn't a reason for it, despite Abby being convinced that the drivers were drunk. I agree there was reckless driving but I felt very strongly that you can't blame anything else. The terrible truth is that, for whatever reason, her daughter was killed and I have to live with the effects of a brain injury.

I suppose she probably needed to blame something, to explain the accident. I couldn't carry on arguing and by now I was worn down by her views and the constant contact so I said I didn't want to stay in touch if she was going to blame the accident on made-up causes like drunken drivers. I haven't spoken to her since.

Because of the accident, I have been exposed to people having different reactions to what happened and finding different ways of coping with it. I guess this has made me decide specifically what I thought about the accident myself. I've seen how people can either help me deal with the effects of what has happened or take advantage of it, using it as an excuse for their behaviour or a basis for misunderstandings. As time has moved on, I feel I've become better at coping with the ramifications and more able to deal with everything in whatever way works for me.

People made presumptions about me throughout my recovery. Mostly this was due to ignorant views about the nature of brain injuries, my injury in particular and the way it affected my personality. People seem to find it difficult to understand which aspects of my character are simply more pronounced as a result of the accident and that I already realise these are things I have to overcome. I don't want to be caught up in their negative interpretations of my injury. I feel what I've been through is unique and I feel mostly positive about the nature and extent of my recovery.

Roland, a friend since childhood

In my head there had been a certain poignancy about Ben going to visit Jazz in Haiti. We hadn't seen so much of each other in the preceding months but made a special effort to meet for a proper catch-up before he left. When we said goodbye it was almost a tearful farewell. One of the things we discussed that night was our arrangement for me to stay in his room in Belsize Park while he was away. That's where I was when I heard about the accident from Miles. When he first told me, I thought for a split second he was joking.

I guess a good few weeks passed before I had the opportunity to see Ben when he was back in the UK. I got the train down to Sussex with Morgan and James to go to the hospital. I think we were all pretty nervous. I didn't know what to expect and I didn't know how I should act.

As soon as we saw Ben, it felt like a really positive experience. He seemed to virtually jump out of bed (well, with the help of Theo and his dad, he sort of swung his legs down and tried to stand up). I think he wanted to get a good look at our faces. I remember being happy to think he definitely remembered us and was pleased to see us.

On that first, or maybe second, visit, Ben started to speak a bit. His words were quite faint and whispery at that time, which could make it difficult to understand him. When I did catch what he said, though, I was struck by how normal his words were. You knew it was Ben speaking. The first example of this was probably when the music collection on my phone came up in conversation and Ben quietly took the opportunity to joke about my former liking for disco music.

During one of my visits, Ben seemed confused. He was talking about seeing things at the end of his bed, but there was nothing there. This was all stressing him out quite a bit and he decided he wanted to get his bed out of his room. At that point he came quite close to overturning his bedside table. In the end, I virtually had to shout at him to stop but he did, and it was reassuring that he had listened.

Once Ben was back in Brighton and Hove, he was quickly up for getting out and about. I would borrow my mum's car, and Carats Café near Shoreham Power Station became the initial destination of choice. I guess back then the conversation was a bit limited. Ben would repeat himself and sometimes, to be honest, what he said didn't make sense. That said, I normally felt as though I could tell what he was getting at, even if it was coming out in a slightly incoherent way. A good example of Ben's slightly confusing remarks was the word 'abasanjo'. I think it's now agreed this was his own word for his condition, for the effects of his accident. Another word I remember was 'centrifuged', which, as far as I could tell, was his word for tests being done on him.

After the accident, Ben could be quite rude, or at least blunt. This has seemed to soften with time but he does still have quite a low threshold for others' mistakes and a reputation for being a straight talker. I took his directness as an accentuation of a character trait that had always been discernible in him and his friends (probably me included). Essentially, among good mates, there's always been a lot of taking the piss and showing friendship through the use of insults. I always saw Ben as someone who held strong beliefs and basically said what he thought. I've sometimes wondered if his bluntness since his accident isn't always about anger. Maybe he's just showing a side of his character that used to be less noticeable.

Sometimes, however, he can seem a bit unforgiving. I've said to him (and so have others) that sometimes he needs to spare people's feelings a bit and try to see things from another point of view. For example, he used to get annoyed with people who hadn't been in touch with him since the accident or hadn't seemed to make an effort with him. I sometimes thought those people were maybe confused or fearful about what had happened, or simply unaware. I have asked myself whether Ben has tried to avoid feeling hurt by getting angry instead.

The alcohol issue has been a difficult one. The trouble is, Ben always was a big drinker and so are a lot of his friends. It seemed obvious that drinking a lot was not doing anything for him – it certainly didn't make him less angry. It really was positive when he went tee-total for a while. He's drinking a bit now but it seems more under control.

I've always wondered whether the fact we didn't mention Jazz for such a long time after the accident made it more difficult for Ben to remember her or whether his not remembering her was a form of self-preservation. I guess it's probably a whole mixture of things. In any case, he is starting to remember her now, just little bits. He told me he is happy and relieved to remember Jazz, but not exactly sad about losing her.

Thinking about the future has sometimes been difficult. I've wondered what Ben will do with his life. Will he live abroad? Will he continue to work in the development sector? It seems pretty clear he does still want to make a career in that field. Taking a second master's seems to have helped him to refocus on his skills in that area. I think he would still like to take part in the ODI fellowship programme one day, but he is aware he might not be able to.

Gideon, Roland's brother and a friend since childhood

As long as I can remember, Ben has been one of my brother's best friends, and my childhood is full of memories of them going off to play in the park together. I know now that I took my own friendship with Ben for granted, but I think this was quite natural. I knew we'd always be friends because Rol and Ben would always be friends.

My experience of Ben's accident has so much to do with the effect on the social circles surrounding him, in particular his close friends, on whom the accident had such a devastating impact. When I heard the news, it didn't sink in. I decided to ring round as many of our mutual friends as I could because I was very aware those closer to Ben, especially my brother, would be upset and shouldn't have to continually repeat such painful news. I particularly remember speaking to our friend Eleanor who, I think, was the one who suggested we all meet up. A few days later we were all in the pub and there was such an enormous sense we had to support each other and come together for Ben.

Another friend, Aaron, raised a glass and we all toasted Jazz. I didn't realise then that this would be the only time we'd all collectively say goodbye to her. She'd become part of our lives and I'd assumed I'd always be friends with her. It was only weeks later, lying awake one night, I started to cry.

The summer before the accident we were all at Glastonbury together. I remember sitting in the cabaret tent then wandering around in the dark with them both – all so innocent and carefree. In the few days after the accident I felt incredibly guilty that all Ben's friends and family knew Jazz had died but he didn't. It didn't seem right that I knew something so important to him when he didn't because of his coma. I was struck by the tragedy of his situation because I imagined him waking up and discovering the awful truth. I felt so sad for Ben then.

When he did wake up and begin his recovery, I had no idea he wouldn't remember Jazz. I again felt guilty because it was agreed we wouldn't mention her to him – it would be too devastating.

I went to visit Ben in the hospital with my brother a couple of weeks after he'd been returned home to England. I'd spoken to Roland and Morgan about his condition and so I had prepared myself for the worst, but I was very glad to find him able to chat and share a joke with us. I remember thinking that if his sense of humour was intact, then the damage to his brain couldn't have been too severe. When he lay in bed he seemed almost like his old self but when he got up to go to the toilet he was obviously having a lot of trouble.

I'm so glad Ben has recovered as well as he has, but he's different in lots of ways. Ben was always very clever and kind but also quite a gentle and unassuming character. Everybody liked him. I used to say some horrible things to him just as a joke. We'd both laugh because it was so totally unjustified. It was funny. Since he came out of the coma he has been a lot more outspoken. At the beginning he was often quite rude and I realised sometimes that I was on the receiving end of what might originally have been a joke delivered by me. It was almost as though he'd stored up all those 'wanker' jibes and was firing them back at me.

I do find it strange a person can change so much and still be themselves. I guess that happens to all of us, but not so quickly. I've noticed lately that Ben seems calmer. I know the recovery slows down but I still think he's making progress.

Jenny

Since Ben's accident, Hugh and I have become experts with a very small 'e' – experts in how the impact of his brain injury shapes what he does and how he is. Our professional background as practising psychologists in the field of education and special needs gave us some insight. It made us think about a whole range of things in a different way. That old chestnut of defining what makes us who we are has been a recurring question. We are defined by our memories; what we remember, together with layers of experience, shapes who we are. But how must it be if we have no memories? If we can't remember people and places to understand their connection to us? When Ben had the language to ask us some fundamental questions, such as *Where has the old Ben gone?* and *How do I know you are who you say you are?*, it gave us a perspective of the world he was inhabiting.

Ben told me my always saying it was 'me, Mum', when visiting him all those weeks before he was able to make sense of what he was seeing, gave him a certainty that the voice and face fitted. Much later on, when he wasn't sure who was collecting him for his day-visits home (even though it was always me and his dad), the staff would see me approaching at a distance down the corridor and gleefully say, 'There she is! We told you your mum was coming!' and I would follow by singing out, 'Hi, Ben', with the usual familiarity. I realised that it drew a noticeable reaction from him. Ben's relief that it was indeed me was clear to us all.

Using visuals early on, particularly when talking about friends, was helpful. Sometimes that wasn't enough, but seeing people in the flesh would do the trick and trigger the memory of who they were. However, if the link was more tenuous, then placing them would remain unresolved for him. *How far back had his long-term memory been affected, and how much would he regain?* These were questions that couldn't really be answered, though Ben was frequently asked how far back he could remember. Most things began to layer up through us telling him. But one thing remained elusive: his memory of Jazz.

Language is important in defining who we are and, of course, in expressing our memories and experiences. If you haven't the language, you can't express yourself or communicate other than at the most basic level. If you can't generate the vocabulary, then you haven't the building blocks of language, and without language you are missing the tools of thought. At the beginning, speech was physically difficult for Ben and the hospital speech therapist spent her time helping him establish a reliable swallow without the possibility of choking. She then worked on basic vocabulary by showing him flash cards and asking him to name the object. But before this, when Ben first began to talk, he twittered and whispered unintelligibly to the rest of us. In part this was due to his inability to generate an out-breath to effectively vibrate his vocal chords, but he also no longer had the words to communicate with.

Hugh spent a long time getting him to strengthen his out-breath and then combine that with a word or short phrase linked to telling us what he needed. At the beginning this was all about communicating his basic wants, such as needing a drink, the loo or whatever. As he couldn't just get up and get what he wanted, he needed to tell us. It felt a little like those early days with a toddler who keeps trying to ask for what he wants while the rest of the world is not getting it. So, once we'd ascertained what he wanted, his dad would give him the short phrase, which Ben would confirm as being the right thing, and then he would imitate Hugh with the phrase on his out-breath.

To make our hospital visits more interesting, we all played games with Ben. We marvelled at certain things he did with ease. Did this reflect part of his memory store that remained relatively intact? Was it related to memories within a time-frame that were more resilient and therefore didn't need to be re-learned like most of his skills and knowledge? No one could give us any explanation. A friend brought in an atlas and an evening was spent looking at maps and asking Ben to name countries, capitals or find places he'd been to. Without fail he could do this with ease, much to the glee and delight of those present, who relayed this achievement to us in the visitors' book. We knew he could name the songs and artists on his playlist after hearing the first few chords. I would just love asking him each time who it was. Eventually, after many months, he couldn't believe I was still asking him, and how come I couldn't remember, despite him giving me the same answer every time! Once, driving home, Ben joined in singing a song on the radio, ahead of the timing of the song and totally out of tune, but recognisable and with the lyrics entirely right. We delighted in all of this, which was no less amazing for not having any explanation of how it might happen.

After a couple of years of being back home, Ben discovered his music files on an old laptop and couldn't believe it was his collection. He doggedly transferred them to his current laptop and onto his iPod. His taste reflects the music he was into in 2010 but also links to what he has always enjoyed listening to. This was another discovery that amazed him, and sorting out his music continues to give him pleasure. We do sometimes groan when he gets stuck on a particular CD and plays it over and over again.

Another of the favourite games I often played with him early on involved giving him a list of group nouns, such as farm animals, and asking him if, say, the named animal was indeed a farm animal – *So is a cow a farm animal?*, and so on, until we threw a googly into the mix, such as *Is a shark a farm animal?* At first Ben would continue to say yes to any combination. We would correct him with exaggerated humour: *No, a shark lives in the sea, not on a farm!* with hoots of laughter, which he would readily join in. Over the weeks he began to get it and we progressed to differing classifications, but still only needing a yes or no answer rather than generating his own lists. Could he tell you red was a colour? At first, no. Could he name everyday objects? At first, no. Did he move on to being able to generate common lists of nouns? Eventually, yes.

Ben was always good-humoured and amenable to his therapy, activities or being corrected. At home, he would join in with everyday life, often asking how he might help. Simple tasks were the order of the day. Putting the cutlery away from the dishwasher was an early task that totally flummoxed him. I gave him the cutlery basket and opened the drawer for him to put away the knives and forks, and so on, in the right compartments of the cutlery tray. After a while I noticed him standing there, staring at the tray without a clue as to what to do. The instruction had meant nothing to him, and the full basket with the cutlery drawer open meant nothing to him either. So I took a spoon out, named it and asked him to find one in the drawer like it. However, even then he didn't locate the spoons in the drawer easily. After a few goes, he got it and could match the cutlery in the drawer with what was in his hand.

We always thought he had significant visual perception problems as a result of his accident but, despite raising concerns and asking questions, this was never followed through. His sight had been tested several times and his vision was pronounced fine, as was his tracking from left to right and his up-and-down gaze, but I don't think the tests were designed to detect the perceptual difficulties he had. Taking him shopping and asking him to get a particular yoghurt, for example, was quite a challenge at the beginning as he couldn't make out what was on the shelf or distinguish between all the different shapes, sizes, varieties and makes on offer. He still finds looking for things difficult when they might be there right in front of him.

We practised all sorts of tasks at home: putting things in the dishwasher, emptying it, helping with cooking, pegging out the washing. Some of these he's become master of and as a result is now far more domesticated than he's ever been. Carrying out individual tasks, such as chopping onions, is something he will do methodically, even though it will take him far longer than you or I. However, cooking something from start to finish has required much practice, mainly to get the order of things right. So a cooked breakfast, which Ben remains very partial to, is quite a challenge and more difficult in its timing than one thinks. To begin with, he would start with the eggs, then place the bacon under a too-hot grill while cutting up the mushrooms and tomatoes and, at the end, put the toast on. The smell from the kitchen would soon alert us to the burned result. While he has now got this down to a T, the planning of any new recipe or food routine does need some care and help in organising the timing or sequence of preparation. Cheese on toast, once again, became a favourite after evenings out. So Ben would come in and invariably burn it. As the smell wafted up through the house, the more worrying thought was, *Had he turned the grill off?* There was no going back to sleep until one of us had checked.

I have a lasting memory of Ben in those early days back home, squealing in front of the sink as it overflowed while he was rinsing some lettuce, with no presence of mind signalling he needed to turn the tap off. It still makes him laugh, and I think it puts into context the progress he has made.

Ben

To return to my 'free' summer of 2011... The first momentous thing I did was to go to the Glastonbury Festival at the end of June, just nine months after the accident. I'd been going to the festival for years, since

I was 14, and I'd last been only the year before, with Jazz. Although a huge amount had changed for me in that year, I felt I was re-entering the world I loved by going back to Glastonbury. I got a ticket and Andrew came with me on a free pass, able to attend as my carer.

My parents also went with us. In fact, the first Glastonbury I ever went to was with Dad. This time we decided we'd all go together and share a tepee, which was a fantastic way for me to enjoy the delights of Glastonbury freely and still have the safety net of my parents. Also, a lot of my friends would be working in the Kidzfield with a youth organisation called Woodcraft that goes every year. I used to go with the same organisation myself. I worked in the kids' field a lot and can remember painting myself green as an alien.

Andrew had never been to Glastonbury but was very up for going, having met my friends at my birthday party a month before, where he got more of an insight into my life. It was, of course, a fantastic perk he wanted to take advantage of, too. For me, it was opening his eyes to an area of my life he hadn't experienced before.

We got there on the Thursday, a day before the music started and just long enough to find the tepee, get to know the site and find my friends in the kids' field. It was good to discover how all this quickly revived my memory. I was aware of the fact I knew everything quite well. It was a bit like going home or doing something I knew intimately, and I was happy to be reminded of this.

It was one of those years when the festival was incredibly muddy. It didn't rain much while we were there but it had rained a huge amount beforehand. Because of the vast crowds of people, the ground was soon churned up into a sloppy paste. It looked as though the ground was coated with diarrhoea – gross! Although the site wasn't difficult to get around, you could no longer sit down anywhere, so it wasn't a very relaxing experience. You always needed a purpose and a set place to go unless you wanted to stand for hours and hours, which wasn't particularly fun.

I didn't actually like the main bands that were playing. They were a very commercial bunch: U2, Coldplay and Beyoncé, none of whom I have any interest in. But I knew that didn't matter as there were bound to be plenty of groups I'd enjoy out of the hundreds playing. I remembered one of the stages I really did like was the Jazz World stage, now called the West Holts stage. It gave the best mix of music and had people such as Jimmy Cliff playing reggae, which took me back to the kind of music I used to be into.

Glastonbury was one of the lighter times in my recovery. I was doing something I knew I'd done a lot before and really enjoyed. When I told the rehabilitation team, who worked with me until the end of May, that it was the thing I particularly wanted to do, they were dead against it. I stated again quite plainly that I wanted to go and they shot the idea down, saying I wasn't ready but could maybe do it in a couple of years. This characterised their view on things: there was so much risk, you might hurt yourself, so you couldn't have fun. I was adamant I wanted to go, no matter how pessimistic they were, so one thing Andrew and I made sure to do together was send the rehab team a postcard. I think it said, 'Best wishes from a muddy Glastonbury, Ben and Andrew.' It felt fantastic sending it to them as a *Fuck you!* I really felt if I wanted to do something, I could. It wasn't anyone else's decision. I think if I'd followed all their advice through I would never have done another master's or many of the things I undertook for rehabilitation. This also shows how Andrew supported my view and didn't fall into the trap of baulking at risks. He helped me have fun while recovering, which must be the best way to get over such a horrendous injury.

However, while at Glastonbury I did come a cropper over one of the many risks they talked about, specifically my mobility. Andrew and I were just walking from one gig to another with my friend, Simon, but it was exceptionally muddy. I was walking along the path a few steps away from them and the mud was so thick I got completely swamped and couldn't see my feet anymore. The mud wasn't slurry at this point; it was beginning to dry out, so it was thick and heavy. I'd got through it fine before that but at this point I couldn't move my feet at all: they were weighed down and I had no way of freeing myself – the insurmountable risk the rehabilitation team were perpetually worried about. I had to ask Andrew and Simon to help me as I was completely immobile. This culminated in the amusing situation of me stuck in the mud with two of my friends supporting me upright as I tried to get my feet free from the thick gunge caking them.

So this was the grave danger to me in going to Glastonbury – I don't think it could have been more amusing. My mobility was impaired not because of the lasting legacy of my injury but because of mud. I wasn't the only one who got stuck that year and, as everyone knows, there are often times when you need friends to help you balance rather than leaving you to sink further.

Andrew

'It will be muddy. Remember to bring wellies,' Hugh texted me beforehand. I smiled at the thought of traipsing around in the mud and rain with Ben – exactly what the rehabilitation team didn't want us to do. Actually, they didn't want Ben to go, full stop. *It could be too much, What if he falls?, Maybe it isn't a good idea*, they kept spouting when Ben and I told them his plans to attend. In a way, the more the rehabilitation team said no, the more determined Ben was. The quiet, unassuming lad I'd met at the beginning had become one fearless individual, with a hint of a rebel thrown in for good measure. I now understood what Jenny meant that day in the hall: Ben had certainly shed any passive or diplomatic mannerisms. He had no qualms about saying what he felt or thought at any moment.

When I was with him, I often pondered whether this outspokenness was a symptom of a healing brain or just that Ben was at a point in his life where he had no choice but to speak up, loud and clear. With so many people speaking for him and making choices for him, his voice would have been lost in all the medical red tape and parental care. Whatever it was, he'd certainly lost the social conditioning that most of us cling to throughout most of our lives, though I admit there were times when Ben's blunt and forthright voice made people feel uncomfortable and embarrassed.

Hugh and Jenny seemed to think it would be a good idea for Ben to attend Glastonbury. All his friends were going and, besides, they would be there too. They discussed it with me on numerous occasions beforehand, asking if I thought it was good idea and, if so, whether I would be willing to go with him. Having met most of them, I knew Ben had a great bunch of friends and he needed to start doing normal things again, so it was only fitting he attend Glastonbury with his mates, as he had for many years. At that point (a few months before the festival), Ben had already come on leaps and bounds with his muscle strength and co-ordination, and together we totally believed he could do it. So that was that. We were going – much to the dismay of the rehab team.

Hugh, Jenny and Ben picked me up at 8am sharp and off we went together, wellies, toilet paper and all, ready for almost every contingency. It was my first time at Glastonbury. Jenny had just been once, the previous year, when Jazz had also gone, but Hugh was a seasoned Glasto-goer, attending every year, and Ben had been many times before. He really wasn't fazed by it at all. On the way there, Ben and I studied the line-up in the back seat of the car and picked out the bands we wanted to see, though most of the bands I suggested he either hadn't heard of, had forgotten, or thought were shit. 'Ben, you should accommodate some of the bands Andrew would like to see,' Jenny said. 'They're all shit,' Ben laughed. In the end we got to see a bit of everyone's tastes.

We arrived after lunchtime and quickly unloaded the car. Ben and I made our own way into the festival ground as we had to pick up my special VIP pass as his carer, which allowed us access to elevated areas in the festival so as not to be bothered by the crowds. It was extremely muddy at the entrance of the site, due to all the comings and goings and rainy weather the night before, but as we got further into the festival area, the mud eased off a bit. Ben didn't have much of a problem walking through the mud that afternoon, though that would soon change.

After unpacking and settling into our tepee, we walked around with Jenny and Hugh to take in the massive grounds, grab some food, locate the nearest toilet and find our bearings. The festival had already got into full swing. Lots of Ben's friends were working there so we planned on meeting up with them the following day.

The first day was a somewhat miserable affair. It was windy and horribly grey and dull, and it rained non-stop (in every direction) from early afternoon. However, Ben, trooper that he was, managed to walk around fine, sometimes holding onto my arm for support. We said goodbye to his parents after a late breakfast and went to meet his friends. We looked like a right pair, as his mum had given me a very bright red rainsheet to wear, which in a way was good because not only did it keep me fairly dry but I could also be easily picked out of a crowd if Ben and I got separated. After spending some time watching Wu-Tang Clan and B.B. King on the main stage with Ben's friends, and tucking into a wide variety of foods from all corners of the land, Ben felt tired (maybe from all the extra effort to get through the mud) and we stumbled back to the tepee for a nap.

Around 8.30pm we woke to the far-off sound of Radiohead, the surprise guests of the day. Both of us felt a bit groggy. I stuck my head out of the tepee: it was still miserable outside. But we took off again with a renewed sense of vigour.

That evening U2 were playing, so Ben and I talked about going to see them with his friend. 'No way! U2 and Bono are shit,' Ben exclaimed. He wasn't the only one who thought that. A large group of people had gathered at the front of the main stage, apparently in protest at U2's alleged tax-avoidance antics. In the end we managed to catch the last few minutes of their set.

'I wonder, were people booing U2 for their tax avoidance or because it's Bono up there?' I asked Ben.

'Both! Definitely both,' he replied.

At about half past four, we made our way to the Other Stage to see The Kills perform, accompanied by a few of Ben's mates who'd finished their shift. The day was now glorious and the mud was beginning to dry up, much to our delight. When we arrived at the Other Stage we decided to use my VIP pass and get onto the large raised platform in the middle of the field. Thankfully, the platform was almost empty so the attendants allowed all Ben's friends to join us, basking in the sun. Halfway through the set a couple tapped me on the shoulder and eagerly whispered, 'Who's the dude? Is he famous?' It hadn't occurred to me, but Ben must have looked like a right old VIP. I glanced over to see him reclining back on a portable fold-up chair with a great big smile on his face, while his friends and I scampered around, got him drinks and ushered him back and forth to the VIP loos. 'It's Ben Clench,' I replied proudly, and walked back over to the group, leaving the nosey pair scratching their heads in wonder. We all had a good laugh, especially Ben when I told them what had happened. 'It's probably 'cause he looks like a rocker who's taken too many drugs,' someone said.

The sunshine didn't last very long and by 9.30pm it was back to being a bit overcast. At the Park Stage we checked out James Blake, a performer I'd wanted to see but Ben had never heard of and, amusingly, kept mixing up with James Blunt (someone both of us agreed was 'shit'). So it took some convincing to get him to see James Blake in the beginning. I assured him it really wasn't James Blunt, and in the end he was glad I'd introduced him to some new music he rather liked. We both enjoyed the performance and afterwards agreed we definitely didn't want to see Coldplay on the main stage. However, it was inevitable, and we got dragged over for a short while, much to Ben's annoyance, before we all left to see the end of the Chemical Brothers at the Other Stage, which was totally insane.

The next day we woke early to a lovely veil of warmth around the tepee, something absent from previous days. Hugh and Jenny were already up, busying themselves outside. Emerging from the tent like two yokels dragged through a bush, we must have looked a right sight. Hugh smiled, barely stopping himself from laughing.

'Good night?' he said. I nodded, suddenly becoming aware my

breath must have smelled terrible. I felt bad, not because of my stinky mouth, but because maybe I shouldn't have been letting Ben drink at all. I mentioned it to Ben later that morning as we queued for the toilet. 'Nah, my parents are fine with it,' Ben replied. 'Anyway, I only had a few all day. I know I can't drink a lot'.

We had learned alcohol wasn't good for the healing brain and the doctors had told Ben he shouldn't drink too much, if at all. I'd seen how it could affect him one night in late February. Ben and I had gone to see *True Grit* at the cinema and later went to the Full Moon pub in Brighton. After one pint he seemed fine, but halfway through the second I realised he was getting drunk and when he tried to get up he wasn't so good on his feet. 'Your dad will be here soon,' I warned. He smiled as he told me not to worry, he'd been much worse for wear recently and though his parents had disapproved of him getting very drunk, he wasn't too bad now. Thankfully, Hugh and Jenny picked us up from the pub before too long and took Ben home.

That night at the pub, we had spoken a lot about Jazz and his feelings towards her, if he had any – seeing as he couldn't remember her at all – and also about their accident. His main concern was that his memories of Jazz were not actually his, but everyone else's. 'How I remember Jazz now is what other people tell me about her. It's Jazz from their perspective, not mine,' he explained. I could see that this upset him and it was the first time I saw him express any sort of emotion about what had happened to both of them.

On the third and last day of the Glastonbury Festival, the sunshine had been constant all afternoon and Ben was in his element as we watched Don McLean, Laura Marling and Paul Simon together with Ben's parents and friends. Later, as Beyoncé began her performance on the main stage, the sun was starting to set, everyone was on cloud nine and the whole atmosphere was rather magical. I looked over at Ben.

'Are you having a good time?' I asked him.

'Beyoncé is a bit shit,' he replied.

It was time to move on. Ben's Woodcraft friends took us across the festival site in order to make the Arcadia performance, a kind of sci-fi techno fire show.

It's funny what you recollect from a chaotic and hazy night. As Ben and I walked back to the group, he turned to me and said, 'I just wanted to say thanks for coming to Glasto with me. I appreciate it. And to let you know I'm very grateful you've been working with me these last few months.' I was touched.

We rejoined his friends before heading to the Block 9 and Shangri-La fields. I told Ben along the way to let me know when he wanted to go back to the tepee, as it was well past 2am at this point and both of us were beginning to flag a bit. Later, when we finally decided to head back, we couldn't find our way out of Block 9 for some reason. After what seemed like hours of wandering around in a maze and asking for directions, we finally found our way out and made it back, exhausted but happy. Ben slept like a log that night and so did I.

Ben

Finding myself was something that came naturally, and the process was a huge amount of fun. There is no downside to trying out 'new' things because you used to like them before. Having to rediscover my tastes and interests was like going on an enjoyable journey where you don't quite know what or where the destination is. You just have to see and try things out until you rediscover what feels right. In my case, I was continually reminded of what I used to like by those around me, who served as memory guides for me. This process wasn't anything to be feared, just a wonderful exploration of myself and also what fitted in with the 'new me'. Of course, your tastes and preferences aren't exactly the same, but finding out how they have changed is another good point for exploration.

Another way Andrew helped me find myself was through cooking. We had talked a lot about when I'd been living in Thailand in 2004 and 2005, and I'd reminisced about the food and how it was really good. Andrew got me a Thai recipe book for my birthday at the end of May. It was filled with recipes to cook – all the classic Thai curries of red, green and yellow, and massaman curry.

I remembered the massaman curry was exceptionally good, so Andrew and I went to a local Thai supermarket and bought the ingredients to make it. This was a fantastic thing to do, as it brought back so many memories. I got very excited at the thought of eating this curry, as it was taking us all day to prepare – consulting the book and thinking about what to buy, plus the four-hour cooking time.

We'd bought all the ingredients and followed the recipe to the letter, even though it called for a lot of chilli. Following the recipe was good and it was fun tasting it, but it was exceptionally hot. It was a meal we'd made for all the family, though, so it needed to be palatable – especially as my mum hates very hot things. It didn't matter, though. I'd cooked it and though the discomfort Mum felt was bad, there was nothing to be done. In the end it was Andrew, Naomi and I who actually ate it, all three of us with eyes and noses streaming. In trying to revive old memories of my time in Thailand I'd ended up with a seriously hot curry that made even my eyes water.

Andrew did so much more than just help me do my physical exercises; he took an interest in every aspect of my recovery. He understood the journey I was on and saw how he could enjoy it just as much along the way. He became a good friend.

Thailand and Thai cuisine became a continuing feature of our relationship. Even when Andrew was no longer working with me and was busy working for care agencies, we would still see each other regularly as friends. We would go to a lot of Thai food places in Brighton and meet up for a meal. Other than that, we'd just hang out together as friends, and I got to know his friends and latest boyfriend. I felt we understood each other very well.

Andrew

As part of Ben's rehabilitation, he and I often went into town. We took the bus from Hove to Brighton centre so he could get used to using public transport again. Both of us loved Asian food, so while in town it wasn't uncommon to see us in a Thai, Vietnamese or Japanese restaurant. One afternoon we decided to go to a Vietnamese restaurant. We both ordered a spicy noodle soup and got stuck in when it arrived. Ben, feeling adventurous and rather curious, decided to use every single condiment on our table, including the spicy sauces and powders. His soup, not even half-eaten, became so hot after these additions that his face quickly turned a bright red and he couldn't finish it. We laughed (and Ben spluttered) so much the Asian waitress came over to enquire if everything was okay. Quickly thinking it was more polite to make conversation rather than carry on laughing in her face, I asked if she was from Vietnam and if she liked it here. She looked at me rather strangely and replied, 'I am actually American, though my parents are Chinese, not Vietnamese.'

At that, Ben made a familiar grunting noise which I knew was him trying hard not to laugh. I bit my tongue, my face now as red as his. The waitress luckily didn't take it the wrong way. 'I get that sometimes. Don't worry,' she said, forcing a smile as she walked away. After she was out of earshot, we burst into fits of laughter. '"Are you Vietnamese…?"' Ben said, mimicking me in a soft-spoken tone. I finished up my noodle soup while Ben fiddled with his half-eaten spicy mess and drank copious amounts of water. We left shortly afterwards, leaving a generous tip for our waitress, and legged it from the restaurant, giggling like kids. We lay on the beach chatting for the rest of the afternoon and enjoyed ice-creams. Soon the summer would be over. My time with Ben was coming to an end. There had been talk of attending university in the autumn, something Ben adamantly wanted to do.

To follow your dreams once in life is hard enough, but to do it twice takes strength and courage, and Ben had that in spades. We often discussed his desire to attend university again and complete another master's, the sooner the better. He was certain it was not only the next move to make but also the correct one, for a number of reasons. He'd started talking about finding a girlfriend and believed the only way to meet one was at university. 'All my friends are hooking up together now. Look at Miles and my sister,' he said, licking his ice-cream. It was something he often commented on. 'My accident brought them together,' he reminded me yet again. I sensed Ben was perhaps beginning to feel a bit left out or left behind. He told me in his future he pictured a wife and a life he desperately wanted to get back to and get on with. 'I need to find a girlfriend, Andrew,' he insisted, and that day he was certain that going back to university would be the only way to do so.

Early on in the summer, Jenny had asked me if I thought it was a good idea for Ben to attend a master's course in the autumn. One thing is certain: I never doubted for a second he could do it. He is a determined individual and once he sets his mind on something there is no stopping him. I told Jenny I didn't know the answer to her question because the one person who could answer it was Ben himself. I realised during my time with him that Ben's rehabilitation involves understanding and processing what happened, reaching a kind of no-holds-barred *Who am I now?* moment. Going back to university would allow him to do that. And, of course, it would give him the opportunity to look for a girlfriend.

By September he'd been accepted to Sussex University and our working relationship was coming to an end. Though we planned to stay in touch and meet up regularly, I knew Ben would be busy balancing a whole host of new tasks and most of his time would be devoted to that. Plus, I was planning on doing a master's of my own at Brighton University, studying rehabilitation science at their Eastbourne campus, starting in January. The interview was in the last week of October and the whole year leading up to it had been devoted to work experience and preparation. I was confident enough my time with Ben had not only given me a window into the world of rehabilitation therapy but also some great life lessons along the way, too.

Ben wasn't at all daunted about returning to university and he was confident it was going to work out. In a way, he had what many of us don't: a wonderful belief in himself. Before he started at Sussex, we took the train together up to the university a few times so he could become familiar with the campus and accustomed to the train ride, something he'd be doing alone daily. We visited his course director and the admissions office. They seemed rather excited to have him join the programme. Everyone reassured him he would definitely be supported all the way, which made him feel rather lucky, I think, and he was entitled to a new computer and printer to boot, which made him feel even better.

It's funny how life works out sometimes. What seems hard is very often rather simple and what should be natural comes to seem rather difficult.

'What? Those bastards!' Ben said over a hot chocolate when I told him I hadn't been accepted to join the rehabilitation science course. 'What are you going to do now?' he asked, sounding concerned and a bit like my dad.

'Not sure. Maybe I'll move to Barcelona,' I replied, half joking, and added, 'I'll decide after Christmas.' I took a sip of my hot chocolate.

'Barcelona? Why would you want to move there?' he said, now sounding exactly like my dad.

Guillermo lived in Barcelona. 'I go where the heart is,' I said.

'Just as well. Eastbourne is full of old people, anyway,' he replied, lightening the mood. Ben always had a good way of putting things – bluntly, with a wry smile and a hint of whimsy.

'I guess that's why they have the rehabilitation campus in Eastbourne,' I said. 'To practise on all the old fogies.' We both laughed and ordered another hot chocolate from Guillermo, who was working in the café and hovering nearby.

Ben

Back in that first, post-accident, summer I began to rekindle my love for travelling. In May 2011 I went to Barcelona to visit a friend I'd got to know when I was doing my BSc. I'd visited her there before, years ago, in 2006, just as we'd finished our degrees and were both wondering what to do next with our lives. It was a period of change and flux, neither of us knowing how our lives were going to shape up. Nothing was serious or set in stone – we enjoyed each other's company and when I was staying at her home we simply had lots of fun and also slept together. It was a very casual relationship and neither of us wanted to keep it up. So we got on with our lives. I ended up doing my master's and had other relationships, and I know she did as well.

I'm not too sure how this friend heard about my accident but she did hear, and came to visit me when I was out of hospital. She was very sympathetic and said I should keep in touch through Facebook. So I sent her an email late that spring, just after the neuro-rehabilitation team had left me.

We agreed I'd go and visit her. My memory of Barcelona was of a very picturesque city with lots going on, and while I was there I met some of her friends who I'd met all those years ago. This trip was all about reconstructing my life and reviving experiences I'd been through before. In fact, it was so like what we had done before that, as she was single and so was I, we slept together just as we had the first time. However, the knowledge of why we used to sleep together, of it being a pretty casual affair, was lost in my damaged memory, meaning I put more emphasis on it than I should have.

Because of this misunderstanding, I expected more from our relationship, not remembering it had always been a casual thing. When I undertook the Brighton Half Marathon some months later, my friends saw this on Facebook and many of them commented on this as being quite an achievement. I also thought it was a big leap, one that showed my continuing commitment to recovering from the accident. Although a lot of people left messages, my Barcelona friend didn't say anything. I took this as a deliberate and hurtful snub, and decided to remove her from my Facebook friends.

A few months later she told me she was coming to England and would be happy to see me, but she explained we could no longer sleep together as she was seeing someone. I told her I didn't know whether I'd see her, as she'd never said anything about my half-marathon, which is why I'd deleted her from Facebook.

So she didn't see me that time she came to England, but she did accept me as a friend on Facebook when I added her back some months later. On reflection, I feel this was a simple misunderstanding, where I was reading far too much into things. The failure to remember our previous relationship was a serious mistake on my part and one I don't expect to make again.

Another face from my past resurfaced after my accident. I'd lived in Berlin for a year doing an internship, and one of the women who knew me there got in touch during my recuperation. She said she'd heard about my accident from my friend Campbell, who'd kept people informed about my progress since I'd been in hospital. She asked if she could come and see me and my family in Brighton, which was fine, although I couldn't actually remember her. (As it turned out, she hadn't been working for the same company as me – she just knew me through various other people who worked there.)

She came to visit and it was nice to see her, though I still didn't remember how I knew her. But we stayed in touch and her world seemed like a forgotten side of my life I was keen to get back. She was still living in Berlin and was still in contact with a few people I knew from my time there. As a result, she invited me over to refresh my memory of the city. I took her up on this offer in the summer of 2012, while I was just finishing my master's, the taught course behind me and only the dissertation to complete.

Going to Berlin refreshed my memory surprisingly quickly and effectively. I recognised so many places and met lots of people I'd known before. It was an excellent retracing of my earlier experience and a brilliant trip for retrieving the memories lost in my brain. It was an interesting trip, too, because my friend and I began a relationship and I was hopeful we might continue it. I felt I'd come such a long way by that point and was getting on much better socially.

Unfortunately, it didn't work out, partly because she was incredibly critical of my behaviour. It seemed she couldn't cope with my forgetfulness and the fact I quite plainly said what I thought. These were two effects of what had happened to me. It felt terrible she was so critical of me, yet had invited me over to Berlin and even slept with me.

After the trip, I endured months and months of misunderstandings as I tried to work out what was going on and how things had gone wrong with the relationship. Finally, talking to friends helped me put this damaging relationship behind me. I realised I needed to bar her from my Facebook and Skype and never have contact with her again. It seemed that she was quite manipulative and it wasn't worth putting in the effort to remain in contact with her. The decision to not have contact with her again has made me a much happier person.

In September 2011, my family went on holiday to Corsica. Theo and Naomi came too, as everyone really wanted to be away and together at that particular time: it was exactly one year since my accident. It was supposed to be a break for all five of us, to mark how far we'd all moved on since those dark days when I was in a coma. It was also a chance to spend time together before I was due to start my master's at Sussex University.

The trip fell at an in-between stage of my recovery. Through Andrew working with me, I had regained a lot of my independence and re-learned how various bits of my life fitted together, and been to Glastonbury to rediscover my music interests. I needed to be able to process and consider information and ideas, which is why I was going back to university.

So this holiday came at a critical point in my recovery. It was in a very nice place, extremely beautiful and where most people speak French, which Mum is fluent in. My parents hired a villa and a car so we could explore the island, and we spent a lot of time driving around to enjoy the sights and glorious scenery. The island is French and to me it didn't seem that different or exotic, although the Corsican separatists would disagree as they'd claim it's nothing like France and its own place entirely. However, it feels French in its customs and food.

Given this, the trip to Corsica wasn't very thrilling. We have been on some pretty crazy family trips, such as when I was living in Thailand for a year and Dad took me to see the komodo dragons in Indonesia, which was as adventurous as it comes. By contrast, this holiday was supposed to be a time to relax and reflect.

However, I wasn't very relaxed and really felt my injury was a ball and chain around my neck as I still had so much more to do to recover and shake it off. So it wasn't a very comfortable time for me. I was feeling the weight of what I had to do. It was daunting and scary and I knew I was heading for a fantastically difficult period of mental rehabilitation. Because of this, I really wasn't very interested in the place we were visiting. I knew I had the master's to do very soon and was pre-occupied with that. I had a lot of stress and was not in a very good mood.

I remember Corsica as some time out, but not your typical easy-

Ben and I on Komodo Island, Indonesia, next to one of the smaller dragons (with a radio collar), August 2005

going holiday. I get the impression my family think this, too; that it was not a carefree time for me and I was behaving like a teenager rather than an adult who was nearly 30. I was in a bad mood and snapped a lot, particularly at my sister. There was nothing I enjoyed, other than complaining about what we were doing or about my family's behaviour. I imagine I must have been a nightmare to be around.

Sadly, I don't remember anything positive about that holiday – only the pressure I felt under to keep on going with the arduous climb up the mountain to haul myself to where I had been before. It wasn't something that was going to be easy or particularly do-able, but that was the only way I was going to do it.

In order to reach that point, where I could truly contemplate work again, I'd had to pre-occupied my brain to cope with the rigours of analytical thought. So the summer of Glastonbury and Corsica also saw me begin the application process, which culminated in my starting university to do a second master's.

I'd done a huge amount that first year, working on my fitness

Ben and his mum, Corsica, September 2011

and memory and sense of self, and I'd re-learned so much. The one big problem was I hadn't worked much on my cognitive abilities and stretching myself mentally. I knew I would have to do this if I wanted to regain myself fully. With the help of my dad, I visited the Institute of Development Studies (IDS) at the University of Sussex to discuss ways in which I could access some learning related to international development in order to rehabilitate cognitively.

Here I saw the head of the governance and development course and we talked about me attending some lectures to get my mind back into the way of thinking in the world of international development. The course tutor was very supportive of me doing this and suggested I start at the same time as the new intake for the course in September with a view to trying the full master's or, if that proved too much, aiming for a diploma instead. I felt this would be a good way to see how I took to the rigours a university course would demand and we agreed I would start university, for the third time in my life, in the autumn.

Rebuilding My Brain

The fact he's completed a master's and worked in an office is incredible. I remember sitting with him in his living room soon after he'd got home and he didn't believe he'd ever read again.

Robbie Barkell, a friend of Ben's and Jazz's from LSE

*

Jenny

By the summer of 2011, just nine months after Ben's accident, his therapy programme had come to an end. Andrew would be moving on and Ben's routines and structure of the past months would need to be replaced. Being busy and at times full-on seemed to be what suited him. But *Busy with what?* was the big question.

Friends and relatives with experience of health services abroad were surprised at how quickly support and input had come to an end, particularly against the backdrop of evidence about the time the repairing brain needs after trauma. Nothing I've read has suggested that less than a year is an optimum time to withdraw help. In the Dominican Republic we'd been told the first 12 months would see Ben make the greatest progress, with a slow-down in the speed of change in the years that followed. This has been so.

However, at that point, nine months on, Ben was still having problems finding the right words for things, his reading was really slow and best done when he closed his left eye, and he found it difficult and frustrating to write using a pen, a task he often chose to avoid. So when Hugh came up with the idea of his going back to university, my first reaction was one of sheer horror. The man was deluded and unrealistic, and what message were we giving Ben about pursuing something that would be beyond him intellectually and might not lead anywhere?

I came home one evening to the news that Ben and Hugh had had a meeting with one of the postgraduate course leaders at Sussex University, Diana Conyers. Moreover, she'd said Ben could join one of the master's courses on offer within the Institute of Development Studies (a postgraduate department at the university), in International Development, in September, with the agreement his place would be reviewed over the course of the first term to see whether he was coping or not. Her generous offer was made on the strength of Ben's CV which, while an impressive summary of his achievements up to the time of his accident, was of little relevance to him now as he couldn't remember what he'd achieved or contributed to during the various positions held. What's more, his overall abilities were still considerably impaired, whether physical, cognitive or relating to his use of language or his reading and writing skills.

We hoped that through reconnecting with a subject that had been important to Ben over many years, there would be many positive spin-offs for his continuing progress. At that early stage we had no expectations of him completing the course with a master's at the end of it; just taking part would be brilliant. It would help him engage his brain and stretch him intellectually. There might also be other pluses for him: a new and different social context, the possibility of friends who hadn't known him before the accident. Who knew what this new experience might bring?

Before term started, Andrew and Ben planned the journey he'd need to take every day and took the bus out to the university, locating the building where his course would take place. They soon decided the train would be quicker, even though it was not a direct route. So that journey was practised. They located the student union building, the library and other key places, and the best way to and from the campus station and the postgraduate school. Angie, who was still coaching him in voice projection and speaking clearly, helped him practise introducing himself in readiness for those initial encounters.

The neurologist who'd taken on Ben's case at this stage had recommended a psychological assessment. We thought this had been done while in hospital but, as no record could be found, he thought it might be worth doing. A hot afternoon was spent at the regional neurological centre, where Ben carried out the various elements of the assessment. We came away with three key points. The first thing the psychologist told Ben after the testing was that, while his cognitive functioning was impaired, he was fortunate because his high level of intellectual ability meant he still had more than he would if he hadn't been very bright before the accident! The second message was to warn him he would get very tired taking on this course, and this might not be a good thing. We added our own final point, which was that the lack of advice or recommendation was regrettable and remains the most long-lasting impression of the assessment.

However, we did have a good laugh on the way home, as the assessor had mentioned that when she asked Ben to repeat a short story to her, he had simply made up his own. Rather than say he couldn't remember it, his explanation had been that he preferred to offer something approximating what she'd requested.

The psychologist's report was later copied to Ben. It turned out much of the assessment was invalidated because on most test components or tasks he ran out of time and didn't get a score. However, where he didn't need to talk or be timed, he was a good average in non-verbal problem-solving tasks, and that was sufficiently positive feedback for him.

As autumn approached, when people asked me what Ben was doing, I usually just said he was going to take a course at the university. That in itself was quite brilliant and beyond any expectation 12 months before, but to say he would definitely be doing a master's seemed at this stage rather premature.

When the start date arrived, I felt more anxious and apprehensive than I had at any other landmark. I thought of him on and off all day, wondering how it was all going. He was starting something with no one dedicated to support him and without anyone really aware of all his difficulties. Hugh and I were both home before him and there was some relief when we heard his key in the door. His heavy steps were an indication he was knackered. In he walked, exhausted, with his name sticker still on his T-shirt and food stains all down his front and bag.

'Well, how was it?' we asked. 'Good,' he said. But after a few more questions we learned he hadn't managed to carry his lunch tray as well as his bag, so he didn't get to sit down outside on a grassy bank in the sunshine with the others. Well, of course he wouldn't have done and, we realised, neither would he have thought to ask someone to carry his tray or to help him. The meal had slipped onto him, nearly covering those already seated. He said someone had come to the rescue, but I'm not sure he got any lunch. The team-building activities hadn't gone too well, either, as he'd been asked to tear up pieces of paper for others to distribute and then been told off for being too slow. We were shocked. This was university! The message about Ben hadn't got around. While the lecturer concerned was, Ben told us, some big name in the development field, Ben felt the man's impatience was of greater significance than his esteemed scholarship. 'Twat,' was what Ben thought...

After a while, Ben managed better, got himself organised and spent most of his waking moments reading for his coursework and preparing the expected assignments. When he wasn't at home, his time was taken up with seminars, lectures and sometimes additional events organised by the development department. The course was keeping him fully occupied and stretching him well beyond what the rehab team or the psychologist would have approved of. He was totally immersed and focused, with little time for anything else apart from his gym sessions with Alex, which he kept up, and the Tai Chi he'd begun that autumn.

The course administrator was fantastic at responding to his queries, usually about something he had forgotten. His early written work, which didn't count towards the overall course mark, was marked with some leniency by his tutor. The fact he produced anything was, to us, a miracle. She apparently admitted to him later on she wasn't too impressed. His typing was really slow but he hadn't forgotten the quick tips and short cuts of the function keys. However, we noticed he had fallen back on his previous way of studying, which had relied on his once-excellent memory and on absorbing huge amounts of information with the ability to reproduce it to suit the assignment. This style of working was not helpful but changing to adapt to a different method was too difficult for him.

We later learned that if Ben had strong opinions he lapsed into using offensive language, which some lecturers handled better than others. I'm sure some of the students accepted him better than others, too. Ben realised his being allocated to a seminar or project group was not always positively received by the other students. And I don't blame them. However, there was one occasion when the communication between a group and Ben was so lacking that he hadn't been included in the discussion, preparation or planning. He hadn't even realised he was part of the group until the morning of the presentation. He told us how totally awful the entire experience had been for him, standing in front of the whole group, including lecturers, and fumbling his way around something he couldn't deliver. While I really felt for him, his reflection on the whole experience showed how far he had come. Just a few months earlier, I'm not sure Ben would have been able to reflect on how awful it had been. He might have laughed or walked away saying *Fuck you*, and it wouldn't have mattered to him too much. But this time it did.

Hugh discussed with Ben's tutor the possibility of having someone or a few peers from his tutor group who could just check if he'd clocked who he was working with before it was too late. Without any allocated help from the Student Support Unit, which was supposed to provide assistance to students with special needs, this was a solution that could have been a good one but didn't materialise, and nor did Student Support, despite our repeated enquiries. Ben wasn't dyslexic, nor was he in a wheelchair, nor sensory-impaired. Thus he didn't tick the right box and when the allocation of a support tutor did happen, months into his course, it didn't provide much that was helpful to him, so he decided to do without. However, he did qualify for technology support, so he got a computer, printer and scanner, but never had the additional training to help him access software that might have been of help to him.

Hugh's endless patience provided Ben with the most effective support. Sunday nights were spent ensuring he had all the papers and reading material printed out in readiness for the week's learning. Putting these together, filing them in the right folders and identifying which were linked to which lecture, seminar or tutorial, took some doing. But Ben finally got the hang of it and organised himself without our help. We got good at proofreading his essays and helping to arrange his thoughts, pointing out where he'd repeated himself or where he'd written rubbish. Self-correction was never something he did spontaneously and the best way to point things out was to get him to re-read what he'd written. The errors were then obvious to him but checking was not a habit that became established. It felt like going back 10 or 15 years, getting irritated about the kids leaving homework to the last minute on a Sunday night.

After the first term, Ben and Hugh met with Diana Conyers and between them they agreed Ben would benefit from continuing. He had made a lot of progress and was obviously getting lots out of it. But perhaps he should he do the course over two years instead of one, or think about a diploma? Ben's usual direct response made it clear to all he would not make any compromises. He wanted to complete the course in a year and strive to get another master's.

Six months in and Ben chose to do largely without our help. He had found others to support him. His work was marked without any allowances and consistently passed. I know Ben was sometimes disappointed his marks weren't higher. Was this going to be a pattern? Never getting to fulfil his high expectations?

He spent the summer on his dissertation and, with some editing support provided by the department, he passed. Amazing, fantastic and beyond anyone's expectations, all down to his dogged determination, strong self-belief and a good dose of his 'fuck you' attitude. That year also gave him a purpose, a goal and a sense of belonging, which would all have to be found as part of the next step to become 'Ben' again.

Ben

Taking part in the master's course was an intense form of mental rehabilitation. It was very difficult and absolutely exhausting but it was something I knew I had to do to recover well. Through doing it I overcame several challenges, the first of which was being so exhausted simply through going to campus regularly. After being in class all day

I'd get home totally wiped out. I was so tired I'd fall asleep straight away from using my mind so much.

I remember having to do all the essays expected of me, and Diana, the programme leader, being really quite concerned as to whether I could do a full master's. I was adamant that as my parents were paying for me to do the course I had to do it. Having been given so much opportunity, there was no way I wasn't going to prove my gratitude by completing the course.

The first term hit me the hardest. I was so pleased I was living at home and had my parents to make me eat and had a nice bed to sleep in, because there was such a lot I had to do to keep my head above water. Just keeping up with the timetable and making my brain work to the maximum was horrendously taxing. Those first few months were utterly draining but it turned around soon afterwards. I wasn't so tired and it became possible to keep up and not fall asleep as soon as I got home every day.

It was also a good experience for me to be in the class and deal with other people, so it was helpful social rehabilitation after the long months of being stuck at home and only having daily contact with my family, Andrew and the NHS therapists. I originally told everyone in the group what my situation was and why I was there. I think this was the best thing to do, laying it on the line from the very beginning. All the other people on my course were very accepting of this and they could see how much effort it was for me to get back to studying.

Throughout the first week we had various social activities to get to know the other people on the course. On the first day we all had a curry lunch we could eat outside on the grassy knoll next to the building. We each collected our curry and went to sit in the sun. However, I was still poorly co-ordinated and fell over, dramatically spilling curry all over me. One of the other students helped me clean up – I had curry all over my neck and over my belongings on the grass. This incident perhaps suggests it was too early for me to go back to university but I was determined to do all I could to counteract the negative effects of the accident. Doing another master's so soon afterwards shows my desire to overcome them. One embarrassing curry incident wasn't going to put me off. And my fellow students were always understanding.

It was a disappointment I wasn't supported as much by the lecturers, who would just forget about my situation. No matter how many times Diana reminded these people what had happened, they would still forget sometimes. The professors often asked me why I was shaking my head; why was I agreeing or disagreeing with what they said. Then I'd go and speak to Diana, absolutely furious I was getting this embarrassing attention in front of the whole class. She had to remind each lecturer just before they taught me again, so they didn't have this totally insensitive reaction to my head-wobble.

It was the opposite end of the spectrum from the NHS and from other organisations like the brain injury charity Headway, which can be too focused on disability, to the extent where you lose your autonomy because of the way they view the problems you are having. Many university staff, on the other hand, were not savvy about disability and, unfortunately, this caused some problems.

However, it was through going back to university that a lot of my memory returned. I remember being in a seminar and we were talking about this professor from Oxford University. I thought I recognised the name and somehow remembered he was a total bastard but didn't know why. I asked someone I was sitting next to why I remembered him and was having such a strong reaction to the name. The other student's response was, 'No, he's from Oxford, so he must be good!'

At this, I stuck my hand up and the tutor asked me if I had something to say. I said, 'I recognise that name and I remember he was a bastard but I don't know why.' Her response was very good. She said, 'Yes, Ben, a lot of people would agree with you.' I felt vindicated but also it was proof things were coming back to me. I desperately needed evidence to reassure myself that my memories were slowly resurfacing.

This whole period was a great challenge and involved retracing all the skills I used to have and re-learning some of the things I used to be able to do well before my accident. The main value of going back to university was in bringing back my cognitive skills to something closer to how they used to be.

The more formal interaction with my university course mates involved not only the initial presentation we each gave on ourselves, but also a number of group presentations. This was fine for me in principle, but a serious problem was my memory, which wasn't very good at the time. The public speaking wasn't an issue as I wasn't shy in this regard. I was more worried about remembering what I was going to say. Doing presentations in seminars was difficult. When I had to remember what someone said and why, I would easily get lost in the detail.

There were several instances where I was asked to form a group with fellow students to present on a subject. The first of these I cannot remember distinctly but I recall we had to introduce the topic we were to cover that week. This was my first attempt at doing a joint presentation with others on the course, who were students from all over the world. It was within the first few weeks of term, so we hadn't fully got into it yet. I was with two guys from Pakistan and we discussed how we were going to talk about the topic fairly generally and what each person was going to cover. We went with this approach, which we expected was going to cover all the points we needed to raise. However, the desperate problem was my lack of memory, as I would forget the argument and the point I was trying to make, along with the significance of it. This first presentation had so many holes in it.

I was distinctly aware of this and that it was something I needed to overcome. I had to minimise the problem as much as I could, so in the second and third presentations I tried to be very clear about the difficulties that relying on my short-term memory could pose. When I had to do other presentations, my parents suggested I invite my group round for dinner so we could talk about it and make sure they were also clear on the issues they had to be aware of, so more preparation – with contingency plans for any memory lapses – could be carried out.

The next presentation I did was with a German student who came to dinner so we could work out some of the problems we might face. Discussing it was a good thing and we managed not to fall into the same difficulty created by my short-term memory last time. However, my problem seemed to be more of an issue for him personally, as he was worrying about the effect it would have on his grade.

The final presentation I had to do saw me partner a Nigerian girl. We were expected to visit a market in Lewes and provide an assessment of how groups of local farmers had formed, working together to sell their produce, and how they overcame some of the challenges that forming such a group can pose. In many ways we needed to undertake a power analysis of the group and their role in relation to the other groups they came into contact with. This proved a bit too much of a technical challenge for the girl I was working with, so she opted to let me do the power analysis and she did some simple descriptions of how the group was organised.

She came to my house as well and, as we talked about things, we touched on the fact I didn't have the support of the university in helping me organise things. She then offered to support me herself, which I agreed to, to see how it would pan out. My main problem was I needed to organise the reading I would have to do, and get hold of any texts I struggled to find, so as to be prepared for the next week. It always turned out this was a difficult and immensely frustrating thing to organise. It was something I actually needed help with, but instead my coursemate would phone me every morning and ask if I was awake and up, which annoyed me intensely and wasn't something I wanted or needed.

Unfortunately, this misunderstanding made our arrangement a fruitless exercise and unsupportive to my learning. The university was incredibly slow at sorting out study support for me. To their marginal credit, in the last term they did supply a study supervisor who helped me organise my reading for the fortnight, but that was the kind of support I should have had at the beginning.

Diana, Ben's Sussex University course leader

I first met Ben in August 2011, when I was working at the Institute of Development Studies at Sussex University. I was responsible for the overall administration of a one-year master's course in governance and development. My role included the admission of students and their pastoral care, as well as some teaching. Ben and his father, Hugh, came to my office to discuss the possibility of Ben attending some classes on this course.

Ben already had a master's degree in development management from LSE. However, he and his father thought attending some classes at IDS might help his recovery process, including helping him to stimulate his mental processes, recall his previous professional interests and skills, and socialise with like-minded people. We discussed the various options and eventually decided that even though he didn't need another master's degree, it might be best if Ben enrolled to do the full course. We were all aware we were taking a risk; we didn't know whether Ben would be able to cope with the work or what implications it might have for the overall management of the course. However, we agreed to give it a try to review the situation at the end of the first term.

There was a particular reason why I had no hesitation in accepting Ben onto the degree. In April 2010, my husband had a major stroke and he spent the next four months in the same ward as Ben. We worked out Ben must have arrived on the ward only a few weeks after my husband left, and I still had vivid memories of his stay there.

My husband's situation was very different to Ben's. Like most of the patients on the ward, he was an old man (88 at the time of the stroke) and it soon became evident he would never make a full recovery. He was moved from hospital to a nursing home, where he eventually died.

However, there were also two young men, much the same age as Ben, in the ward at that time. One had had a stroke and the other was suffering brain damage following an accident. I was very moved by their situation. At the age of 88, serious health problems aren't unexpected but it's totally different when someone is in their twenties. Both these young men left the ward shortly before my husband did. The stroke victim had made little progress and was moved to a nursing home, but the one who'd had an accident made a dramatic recovery and moved back to his parents' home. I was struck by the similarity between his case and Ben's, including the extent and speed of recovery and the support provided by his parents.

It was evident from the start that Ben would experience some problems on the course and that some special arrangements would have to be made. Dealing with these problems was an ongoing process, which began before the course started and continued throughout the year. It was very much a learning process.

When I met Ben just before the course started, I explained that in the first session all the students would be asked to introduce themselves. Ben suggested this would be a good time to explain his position, including what had happened to him and the nature and extent of his current disabilities. I supported this and admired him for having the courage to do it. The strategy worked well. All the students were aware from the start and therefore less likely to ask awkward questions or be taken by surprise by anything unusual in Ben's behaviour. For example, he warned them (as he had warned me) one of the effects of his injury was he didn't mince his words – he said exactly what he thought about individuals or situations, irrespective of any offence this might cause.

As far as I'm aware, there were no major problems with the other students. At no time did any of them make any negative comments or complaints to me about him. When I asked Ben about his relationship with them, his views were positive. He didn't hesitate to express any opinions he might have about them (for example, to tell me so-and-so is 'a bit of an arsehole') but these were minor irritations, not serious problems.

The teaching staff were a different matter. We had agreed I would tell them about his situation, so they'd be prepared and make any necessary allowances or arrangements. However, at IDS, students are taught by many different staff, some of whom take a number of classes, while others take just one or two. At the beginning of the course, I warned those staff most likely to teach Ben, but several had forgotten the warning by the time they came to teach him, and I forgot to brief some staff who only taught the odd session.

Ben didn't hesitate to let me know when this caused problems. But as the year went on it happened less, mainly, I think, because his disabilities became less evident (for example, his head-shaking decreased and his speech improved), but also because he became less sensitive – and less angry – when an incident occurred.

All the teaching staff were very supportive. No one questioned my decision to enrol Ben and, when made aware of his disabilities, they all made an effort to provide any extra support he might need. The best example, perhaps, was his dissertation supervisor, who went out of his way to help Ben in all stages of the work, from formulating his topic and identifying relevant literature to drafting individual sections. When the supervisor was appointed, I said I was willing to provide any additional support Ben might need, but because of the extra amount of time and effort the supervisor put in, this wasn't necessary. All I did was to help Ben find someone to assist him with the final editing. This is a legitimate form of assistance, which I recommend to anyone who has problems with writing.

There is no doubt that when he started the course Ben was seriously 'academically challenged'. His problems were complex and interrelated, but they fell into four main categories: lack of short-term memory; difficulties in organising his thoughts clearly and logically; difficulties in putting these thoughts down on paper; and, a less serious problem, inability to take notes during classes. The memory problem was critical and, I suspect, contributed to the other problems of thinking and writing clearly and logically. It also created practical problems. For example, Ben had difficulty in remembering when and where he had classes, especially *ad hoc* activities such as extra classes or meetings with his tutors. He also had difficulty accessing his IDS emails and using the online study system, through which all course material is provided.

I was advised by the Student Support Unit that Ben should have a 'buddy'. This person would not only provide academic support but also look after his health and safety (for example, ensuring he got out of the building in the case of fire). I discussed it with Ben and one or two other students who might make good buddies, but the idea never really materialised. By this time, informal support mechanisms within the group were already beginning to emerge and the idea of one specific buddy appeared neither necessary nor practical. As for the health and safety precautions, Ben pointed out to me with characteristic and justifiable indignation, since he'd just completed a half-marathon run he didn't need anyone to help him get out of the building! Somewhat to my surprise, I was able to convince the IDS health and safety officer it wasn't necessary.

The marking of Ben's assignments raised different problems and affected me more directly. I was involved in the marking of the first two: an essay and an exam. Marking is done anonymously, in that the students don't put their names on their papers, just candidate numbers. However, in a course like ours it's often possible to guess who the student is, particularly by the examples they use to illustrate points. In Ben's case, it was easy to identify his work. He made reference to his previous work experience and his exam was typed not handwritten. Moreover, in both cases, his style of writing was quite distinctive. The information was there but not very well expressed or organised. It was therefore difficult to know how to mark his work. This is a problem I face all the time, because many of our students have writing problems, especially those for whom English is not their first language. But it was particularly difficult in Ben's case because of the causes of his problems. Fortunately, I didn't have to decide alone, because two people mark every assignment. He ended up with a C-grade for both pieces of work, which was perhaps slightly higher than he might have received if there were no extenuating circumstances, but only marginally so.

I was not directly involved in marking most of Ben's other assignments. However, I made a point of finding out what marks he received. To my relief and pleasure, he got at least a C-grade for all but one of them. This was particularly encouraging since in most, if not all, cases they were marked by people who didn't know enough about the students to be able to identify them. The assignment where he did not do so well was a paper written in the third term, where it seems he'd misunderstood what was required. I was one of the markers for this and I had to agree it didn't merit a pass grade. This was a disappointment for Ben because he felt, justifiably, the quality of his work had improved significantly over the year, and he wasn't aware of the particular problems of this paper. However, he didn't complain or get angry about it, which was an indication of the other ways in which he had improved over the year.

The best news of all – for me, anyway – was that he was awarded a B-minus for his dissertation. The dissertation was the biggest challenge for him, because it required a higher degree of comprehension and analysis. There is no way he could have written it when he joined the course. He received a considerable amount of support in the writing, both from his supervisor and from a former student he employed to edit it. However, this level of support is admissible and available to all students if they need it. Moreover, although it enhanced the final quality of the work, it didn't reduce the amount of effort Ben had to put into it. His dissertation mark was a major achievement and a very clear indication of the amount of progress he made since starting the course.

The topic of the dissertation is significant. He decided to write it on Rwanda, the country he was about to go and work in when he had the accident. The process of writing the dissertation helped to rekindle both his interest in the country and his understanding of it.

In my view, Ben's year at IDS was a great success. There is no doubt his abilities increased dramatically in the course of the year, including his physical and mental abilities, his social skills and his general ability to cope with day-to-day life. I have no doubt that, whatever he'd chosen to do during that year, he would have continued to improve, but I'm equally confident that attending the master's course played a part in his recovery. As we hoped, it stimulated his mental processes, rekindled his knowledge of, and interest in, development-related work and enabled him to mix with people of similar age and interests. In short, it helped re-open a door into the sort of life Ben was living before the accident, and to which he was, and still is, so committed.

What impressed me most about Ben over that year was his positive attitude. I never heard him grumble or show any sign of self-pity. He was always cheerful and optimistic, looking forward rather than back and focusing on the positive things he'd achieved rather than the hurdles he still had to overcome. In this respect, he was a lesson to us all.

Ben

I came out of the master's achieving a B-minus for my dissertation, which I think is a huge achievement given that two years earlier I was in a coma for a month, no one knowing whether I would survive or not. I feel it really shows just how much can be achieved through willpower, plus a huge amount of support to get you through dark and messy places.

The result was something I was extremely proud of. It felt a little like my achievements were coming full circle. Having worked so much on myself up until this point, I thought that the next step – getting back into work – should be fine. I'd come this far, after all.

Eduardo, a friend from Sussex University

I first met Ben on the first day of our master's course. That day all the students had to introduce ourselves to the class. To be honest, I was a little bit nervous because I didn't feel very comfortable speaking English in public. Ben was sitting in front of me and he looked very serious. His way of looking was very deep. Ben's presentation was very impressive for me. He spoke about his accident and the death of his girlfriend. The story was very dramatic but Ben didn't look for compassion. Simply he wanted to explain his situation. Also, Ben spoke about the challenges he had to face for his recovery during the master's.

At the beginning of the course, Ben had real problems in getting his ideas across but his points of view were strong, which showed he had a strong character, and I think this strong personality was key for his process of recovery.

I don't know how Ben was before the accident. One day he showed me some pictures of him with his friends, from before that time. He looked like a very funny guy and I couldn't help thinking how tough it was for him to overcome all the consequences of the accident and to try to get back to 'normal' life.

During the master's, I had a good relationship with Ben. We often talked about his progress and I tried to encourage him. What I admired most about him was he never complained about his problems. I think he is a very inspiring example for anyone: in spite of the problems you might have, if you fight, you can push beyond your own limits and overcome your constraints in life. I hope to count on Ben's friendship for the rest of my life.

Ben

While I got through my course, I was also keeping up with colleagues at a local company where I'd worked before doing my first master's at LSE. When the course was over, these people were kind enough to offer me three months' work to give me a starting point for getting back on my feet.

However, while it was a generous offer, it proved not to have much substance. They probably didn't have the time to properly think about how they were going to make the idea work and make it suitable for all concerned. I was asked to produce a policy paper about their thinking on climate change evaluations. The consultant who was leading this task seemed confused as to the nature of what he was asking us to do. He basically wanted to look at using an economic theory designed to talk about medium-sized firms to talk instead about climate change and to explore the difference between individual and societal action. The theory was completely at odds with the issue and didn't work in the context. So I was always asking him a lot of questions and saying it didn't make sense, which got a very negative reaction from him.

It was incredibly frustrating because this consultant would then report back to the bosses that I just couldn't get it and was getting confused over minor things, even though he was the consultant and the project concept was his responsibility. I found him as opaque as shit. When I consulted a friend of mine who was doing a PhD on climate change, she said she didn't know what this guy was talking about. However, nobody considered that maybe I wasn't getting it because of the way he explained it. I just said I didn't understand his point of view, which was a reasonable interpretation as endorsed by my friend doing climate change research.

To make matters worse, he would justify himself by saying he understood what my problems were. He had a sister who was kicked in the head by a horse and lost all her teeth, so he would say to me he knew all about head injuries. No doubt her accident was a terrible experience for her, but it wasn't remotely similar to mine. He told me his sister was very needy after her accident. So whenever I asked, quite reasonably in the circumstances, for further guidance, he would put it down to my being 'needy' because of my injury.

So this experience proved a false start and in the end they cut me off completely as a failed effort but no doubt thinking they had tried. I think the main problem was simply that what I was supposed to do was not clearly defined. This is a problem I have had to deal with a lot, post-accident.

Nevertheless, I was back in the game. I'd successfully completed a second master's and had begun to look at work opportunities in my chosen field. It's not surprising it wasn't going to be an easy transition but mentally I was ready to try, and also ready to learn from new work experiences with a view to getting back into full-time employment.

Robbie, a friend of Ben's and Jazz's from LSE

I met Ben while studying at LSE in September 2008. I don't remember the exact day, but I expect we met at one of the weekly Friday-night trips to the Knight's Templar pub with the Development Studies Society. It felt like he spent half our pub sessions either outside smoking with Jazz or inside preparing roll-ups to go and smoke with Jazz. On a side note, I remember vividly the night they hooked up, as Ben was meant to be joining Frank and me for drinks later in the evening but he disappeared back to his boat with Jazz and never came out again!

I got to know Ben better throughout the year. He did a slightly different course to me (development management rather than development studies), so we didn't always mix in the same circles. But, being sociable guys, our paths often overlapped, whether it was meeting as part of a larger group or just having a sandwich outside the library together. When I think of those times, I remember how laid-back Ben always was. Living on a boat, and some of the frustrations that came with it, never seemed to faze him. I think of sitting around in the park with Ben, Jazz and others, reading the paper and trying to do the quick crossword; all of us having vague plans to grab some food later but no one anxious about when or where. It felt like a lot of this carefree approach stemmed from Ben, although some of it was just about being students.

Once the LSE course had finished we actually saw more of each other, be it lunch with Campbell (another LSE friend) near St James's Park or drinks in the Princess Louise pub with other former LSE students. Even when Ben went away for work, to Berlin or Nairobi, we'd always reconnect once he was back. We had plans to meet for a pint after he'd been to visit Jazz in Haiti and the Dominican Republic.

The accident was an enormous shock. All sorts of emotions were flying about: sadness about Jazz's death, relief Ben was still alive, and fear for whether he would come out of his coma or not. While we couldn't do anything about what had happened to Jazz, it felt like there was hope for Ben, so a lot of focus went into working out how, or if, we could support his family (although not having met them before, this wasn't that easy). Grieving for Jazz was almost pushed to the side initially, while we waited for more news on Ben.

As Ben's situation progressed there was still constant worry but also a few genuinely ecstatic moments. For example, hearing he'd landed safely back in the UK (albeit still unconscious) felt like a massive achievement that made me want to celebrate, despite all the other conflicting emotions.

The first time I saw Ben after the accident was in hospital, soon after he'd woken up. It was a real shock as I wasn't prepared for how different he'd look: skinnier, paler, frailer. I actually felt rather sick, like I'd been winded. While I knew how serious the situation was, I'm not sure I'd fully taken it on board until I saw him there in a hospital bed. At that stage, Ben didn't know who I was and didn't have enough energy to stay awake for long. Obviously, it was great he'd woken up, but he couldn't stand up and didn't like bright lights, so I was pretty concerned as to how full his recovery would be.

Seeing Ben in hospital wasn't really seeing 'Ben', though, as he was still so disorientated (although he was keen to interact and talk). For me, I only felt as though I'd properly met Ben again when I was able to go to the pub at the end of his parents' road with him for a drink after he'd left hospital. Sitting around discussing whether he wanted to get back into development or not, it was incredible to see how far he'd come in such a short time.

I'd say the best part about visiting Ben in hospital, and then at home (stressful though it was) was that he was always improving. It all became so much more positive as it became apparent his recovery would have a happy ending. One thing that struck me in particular was how driven Ben was to recover fully. Whether this entailed playing with a ball to stimulate his hands after just waking up, walking with support through the hospital corridors, or trying to read the paper or *The Economist* in later weeks, Ben was eager to do it and eager to recover.

Ben has done so much in so little time, I almost forget the accident was so recent. The fact he's completed a master's and worked in an office is incredible. I remember sitting with him in his living room soon after he'd got home and he didn't believe he'd ever read again. It's great those worries proved completely unfounded.

I'm also pleased to see Ben getting his independence back, which naturally he didn't really have in the weeks immediately after his return home. The first time he came up to London on his own to meet up felt pretty special. Being able to organise his social life by himself, rather than through his parents, must be a relief. And it shows how much he has achieved.

I'm also delighted he remains interested in development and international affairs. I know at one point he was questioning these interests, which is probably natural after a major accident in a developing country, but I'd have felt sad if he'd lost interest completely, given it was the basis for our friendship. I know it must still be difficult for Ben as I think he wanted to be living in Rwanda (possibly with Jazz) by now, and he might not feel quite ready to jump right back into the same kind of office roles he did before, but perhaps patience is now necessary.

In short, I don't feel our relationship has changed a huge amount. We still like to catch up over a drink or some food and moan about our old university professors. That said, naturally there's been a few changes. Perhaps mostly just because Ben has needed support from me over the last couple of years, rather than the other way round as it tended to be before. Ben's a couple of years older than me and always seemed several more years wiser. I can remember having a few too many beers with him around Christmas time in 2008, soon after a girl had broken up with me. While plenty of people had already given me the whole *You'll be better off out of it* speech, when Ben did it I actually believed him. I'm not quite sure why that was – maybe an age thing or the fact he was always so relaxed – but, either way, he was able to reassure me. Ben and Jazz ended up filling a sort of 'older-friends' role for me. I went to them for advice and support but they never seemed to need any from me.

I guess things now work more the other way round. Ben needs advice in applying for jobs and I'm more than happy to assist where I can. Understandably, he's not quite as laid-back as he was before the accident (and swears a lot more!), but as things settle down in his life I wouldn't be surprised if he finds it easier to relax a bit. I'm sure I'd be in a much more stressed state than he is if I'd been through everything he has. Plus, although I luckily haven't needed any relationship advice lately, if I did I think I'd still go to Ben.

Having to rebuild your memories can't be easy and I can't imagine how he's done it. But he has. And when we meet now he always asks me about aspects of my life I've told him about previously. I find this tremendously reassuring, as it's a constant reminder of how well he's recovered and that he's able to create new memories with old friends.

I knew Jazz almost as well as Ben. While Ben's recovery has been inspiring, in how he's personally dealt with it, Jazz's death was just tremendously sad. It's very difficult to draw any positives from her loss.

In the months after the accident, once I'd dealt with all the immediate emotions, I thought it would make me a more relaxed person. Ben and Jazz were both so chilled out and seemed to enjoy every moment, and it felt like I should try to enjoy every day in a similar way, especially given such a vivid reminder of how precious life is. However, on reflection, I think I've perhaps become more driven than more relaxed. I'm not sure if that's a good thing or a bad thing, but it's probably about wanting to get to where I want to be while I still can. I guess seeing how much effort Ben has had to put in to his recovery has partly influenced me to put more effort in to my own life and to try to get what I want from it. Compared to Ben, I've had it so easy over the past few years, so I guess I've been inspired to do something with my life while it's going so smoothly.

Ben's progress has also made me consider, in particular, what makes friendships. I'm not sure how much Ben remembers of our time together at LSE but I'm certain he has a sense of who I am and what type of relationship we had. Rebuilding that friendship on more or less the same basis, and seeing Ben's personality develop again, is refreshing as it shows what people can come through.

Every Cloud…

See How Far I've Come

I do find it strange a person can change so much and still be themselves.
I guess that happens to all of us but not so quickly.
Gideon Susman, a friend since childhood

*

Ben

In numbers, my recovery has been remarkable, even if I do say so myself. The accident happened in mid-September and I was mostly in a coma, in intensive care, until 1 November. If we take that as the true starting point of my recovery, I was out of hospital and back home in two months, travelling abroad in five, enjoying Glastonbury in six. A mere nine months after release from hospital, and less than a year out of intensive care, I was studying full-time for a master's degree. I completed a half-marathon 15 months after barely being able to get out of bed in the rehab ward.

Now I'm writing a book. As I write, in a few months' time it will be four years since the accident. It's been an eventful four years and, although much of what is in this book pertains to the first two years of my recovery, the process is ongoing. This book is part of it.

My inspiration to write largely came about through my involvement with a research project at Charing Cross Hospital where they are looking at head injuries. There they did a variety of tests, including brain scans, and Dr Tim Ham, a member of the research team at the time, told me he'd used my scan in a number of conferences and teaching situations. For comparison he'd also showed a brain scan of someone whose recovery had been far less successful, although their scan apparently showed not too much brain damage. He would give a summary of the two patients' progress and ask participants to match the scans with the reported recovery paths. Invariably the poorer progress was attributed to my scan. It was around the time I'd just started my master's and they were surprised I was not only walking but also back at university. It illustrates how brain scans are not necessarily a good indication of the recovery trajectory someone might follow after receiving a head injury.

Dr Ham suggested that my recovery had been such a positive example I should write about my experience to offer encouragement to others suffering head injuries. While my mum and I were amazed someone felt we had something to say that might benefit others, I came away feeling it was something I could do. After putting the suggestion to family and friends, who seemed quite positive about the idea, I then contacted all those who'd loyally supported me and, with my new tenacity, badgered, hassled and generally cajoled them into contributing their stories.

After finishing the master's and my work placement, I didn't worry massively about getting a job to start with. I had a few things to keep me busy and I got some volunteer work for a charity and also a little bit of development work, which was enough to keep my CV fresh.

Fortunately, I haven't had to stress about money too much as I am still in the wonderful position of living at home. All in all, it has been a great time to really reflect on what I have achieved and to acknowledge that recovery will carry on; it will just take time. I feel it is the small things that really matter now, not major efforts like the master's course. I need to focus on the detail. In particular, I need to focus on my ability to work, and to focus my efforts on working on different things from before. Before, my work involved high-profile research on international development. However, my skills now are radically different and I feel that they could be better used working for a small charity and getting away from doing things for big aid organisations. Unfortunately, I have been slow to realise this and have been focusing too much on doing what I used to do.

There are still things I'm trying to uncover about my past and it's great when I finally get confused facts untangled. For example, I saw a friend I'd made when I was at LSE who was a very good friend of Jazz's and I was able to ask him about something I didn't remember properly. I knew Jazz and I had broken up at one point but I had no idea why. It was something my dad used to remind me of – to stop me thinking that the relationship was so perfect that I might never find anyone like her again. It was his way of saying, *You will find someone else, Ben. Don't worry about that now.* I could understand his view but this was something I wanted to get to the bottom of. When I talked to our mutual friend, he told me it was simply because neither of us knew what we were going to do after we'd each finished our master's. So we broke up for a few days before realising we would stay together and make it work.

When I relayed this information to Jazz's mum, Abby, some three years after the accident happened, it was such a relief to her. I'd originally told her we'd broken up for a few days but that I didn't know what had happened – I'd said this when I was in a really bad place and getting regular phone calls from Abby that I couldn't really cope with. Perhaps it had been my way of putting her off calling every week. Anyway, she was immensely relieved and pleased when I emailed her (we still weren't talking by phone then) to say I'd found this out from an old friend who was certain it hadn't been a serious split, just us wondering how our relationship would last beyond our LSE days.

I organised a memorial for Jazz five years after the accident, and after a lot of encouragement from Kiran, Jazz's sister, Abby flew over from Canada for it. I think this was a very good thing for her to do and, after some initial reluctance, she really appreciated coming over.

Something that has interested me, and given me a different way to reflect on what happened to me, is the number of people my accident has affected in positive ways. I suppose it's natural for anyone in close contact with a tragedy resulting in death and long-term injuries to think twice about their own life. The jolting reminder that no one lives forever, no one can predict the future, can hit home hard in those circumstances.

I think I can claim to have triggered two new long-term relationships (Miles and my sister – simply through the closeness that grew between them following my accident – and my friends Becky and Simon) and brought the odd doomed one to its inevitable close. I've also inspired several career changes.

My brutal honesty has had positive effects too. I was always worried about whether I'd been too upfront and too blunt and if I was causing people harm or discomfiting them, but some of the things I said to a couple of my friends in hospital caused them to make huge changes in their lives, which usually did have positive results. I asked one friend who came to see me in hospital if she was still with her boyfriend, which she was. I thought he was a terrible, manipulative shit so I told her quite forcefully to get rid of him, which she has done and I think she is a lot happier. Another friend was really unhappy in her job so I told her to leave it. As a result, she did, and went travelling for a while. The result of these changes in people's lives from my direct bluntness made me proud in a way that I thought would never happen.

Becky, a friend from Ben's internship at Transparency International in Berlin

Ben's directness has had many positive elements. He's not only direct with others, but also with himself. I believe this is related to his determination, even stubbornness, which has helped him to recover and build an independent life. It's a part of his personality that was less obvious prior to the accident but has been valuable to him and to others.

Ben has become one of my best friends. That doesn't mean we haven't had our disagreements. He's challenged me with his direct approach to life and told me the truth when I didn't want to hear it. He is direct but not lacking in empathy – far from it. He's one of the kindest people I know; just a little rough around the edges sometimes. His directness can be embarrassing, but it does get results.

When I first arrived in Brighton, Ben was very interested in my love life. Why didn't I have a boyfriend? Why wasn't I trying to get one? We talked a lot about our past experiences and previous relationships. Very early on he got it into his head I should go out with his friend Simon.

The first time I met Simon, when I went for a drink with Ben, Ben blurted out (admittedly after a couple of pints) that Simon and I should have babies together. This was the beginning of Ben's sustained, unsubtle manoeuvres to get us together, which he made at any opportunity. It was uncomfortable. He worked on each of us separately and teased us when we were together, until finally we did what he told us. Simon asked me out for lunch in November 2012 and we haven't looked back since. It's not the way I would have liked Ben to go about it, but it did the trick. He can be happy in the knowledge that, while he made us both blush more than once, he pushed us in the right direction. I know he's worked magic for other people, too, and I'll always be especially grateful for his cringe-making encouragement and, frankly, great judgement.

We still go to the pub at least once a week and try to have a coffee when I'm not too bogged down with work. We talk about life, love and work, and in more recent months our conversations have turned towards books and ideas. Ben has begun reading more widely and has taken up his old interest in development economics. I used to be the one recommending books to him; now I have a whole list of titles to pursue when I have the time.

The main thing I'd like to say about Ben is that, although he is different since the accident, deep down he's the same. We all change through our experiences, as we should, and when something so dramatic happens to a person it's only right they should change. Difficult circumstances bring out different elements in our personalities. I'm constantly amazed and impressed by the way he's adapted to his circumstances while also being so uncompromising and brave. Ben has never shown any self-pity about what happened to him – quite the opposite. Rather, he's impressed by how amazing and quick his recovery has been, as are we all. This is as it should be. Thanks to Ben's determination and his strength and depth of character, I'm sure there's much happiness and many more achievements ahead.

Yaz, a friend since childhood

When Ben came home to Sussex, I couldn't see him as soon as I would have liked to. Flu, fear and workaholism got in my way. When I did see him, it was like looking at a paper version of him – so thin and unstable. I was pretty scared. The first thing the motherfucker said to me was this: 'Yaz, have you quit your fucking job yet? You hate it. Quit it. Go forth. Make love.' (Ben often tells me to go out and make love now. I know I fail and disappoint his zest for life.)

When he said that, I knew he would be fine. I waited about a year after the accident to tell Ben that his telling me to quit my shit job had had a really strong effect on me. He laughed his head off. He is exceptionally proud of that and, after a beer, he will often crease up and start pointing at me: *I can't believe you actually quit after I said that. Why do you always do what you are told, you stupid bitch?* I, in turn, will also laugh, sometimes too much.

Ben has always been one of my most favourite beautiful people. This may be in part because he is unbelievably good looking, but mostly it's because he has always just been so incredibly awesome and uplifting to be around, and he tolerates all sorts of flakiness on my part (though nowadays he is quite up for telling me when I have taken non-committal too far, and I am thankful).

I reckon I've known Ben since I was around six. He was my sister's first crush (he helped her paint a bucket in class). My mother has always adored him and for some reason thinks he looks like Jesus, to the extent she bought him a freakish gold-plated dish with Jesus on it for his eighteenth. We didn't really become great friends until we were about 15. We spent our free periods at college in the pub and then lying around on the furniture in Habitat talking teenage crap (we did this at university, too – it turned out to be a hard habit to break). He let me live on his boat for a while, and when I went through a funny break-up he came to Spain to hang out with me and drink sangria and eat squid. Ben is a great friend.

We both went to university in Bath, and Ben, being Ben in typical Ben style, was an absolute hit with everyone I introduced him to. This was especially true of my all-female housemates. Even the hardened lesbians threw themselves at him! Ben, however, was brilliantly oblivious to the impact he had on people. In my house, Ben-fawning became a sport and at times it got competitive and ugly. Most 19-year-old males would have exploited this, but Ben was gracious and generous, and would often come round and make the girls pizza from scratch and listen to all their problems for the simple reward of a beer! With Ben, a beer or a good cup of tea will always win you the greatest smile and some lovely conversation.

Ben and I have been going to the cinema a couple of times a month since I moved back to Brighton. I never tell him this, but when he laughs, or huffs with his ragged breathing, or farts loudly with no shame, I always turn to look at him quickly and it makes me happy he is there, making embarrassing noises, knowing they wind me up but not knowing they make me happy in equal measure because sometimes, in those small, insignificant moments, I wonder what I would feel if he were not there. Who would I have tea with?

Ben

During my recovery I had to do many things for what seemed like the first time, although in reality I had done them all before. Often I just needed the courage to try something again.

Before my accident I'd been an accomplished skier; I had been skiing since I was seven years old. With the accident stripping away so much of myself, I didn't know whether those skills were still in me somewhere or if they'd been totally lost. In January 2012, my parents decided to go skiing with some of their friends over a long weekend. I asked whether I could come along to explore how much of the skill I'd lost and to see how much was still there. With some trepidation, they agreed.

When we went to get my skis, the guy at the shop asked how good I was, to gauge how loosely to tighten my bindings (while experienced skiers have their skis very firmly attached to their feet, it is safer for less skilled skiers to be able to kick them off quickly if they get into trouble, hence the looser bindings). We explained my situation, which he was surprised at, and he decided to put the bindings on very loosely. In fact, he put them on so loosely they would barely stay on my feet at all. This meant my skis would fall off even when I was going along normally, not turning or anything. On the first day I was constantly falling over, to the point where I had bruises everywhere, especially on my bum. At the end of the day we went back to the shop and had the bindings tightened up.

After this I could ski properly. For sure, I wasn't as good as I used to be, which was unsurprising, but after a lot of trying I could remember how to parallel turn and my skills were soon coming back.

Jenny

When Ben heard us discuss an invitation from some good friends to join them for a long weekend in the Alps, he asked if he could come too. The friends generously said it would be fine, but I began to think of all the likely difficulties, as well as the responsibility for Hugh and me.

But if Ben asked to do something, our usual response was to say yes unless there was a good reason to say no. And that was how we ended up on a ski slope in January 2013. Ben's first challenge, of walking on uneven and icy ground in ski boots and other winter sports paraphernalia, was okay. He was slipping and sliding but staying upright nevertheless. The only two figures on the nursery slope ski lift were Ben followed by Hugh. So far, so good. He hung in there, got to the top and managed to let go of the pull-lift. Almost without waiting for his dad he was off down the slope. I held my breath and gasped as I looked up. My eyes misted over with the emotion of it all as down he came to the bottom, somehow still standing and manoeuvring the occasional turn. Cue whoops and hurrahs from us, with Ben immediately ready to now take the chair lift to reach more challenging slopes. We managed to negotiate an interim step and agreed to take the next pull-lift, with more speed and up a steeper slope, before embarking on the chair lift. Ben himself might have felt ready, but we weren't! Who would have guessed this was what he would be up to two years after leaving hospital?

Within hours of taking that first lift, Ben was up on the slopes managing very well. Given a little extra help from us, all the things I'd worried about were non-issues. His determination produced enormous effort, leaving him exhausted and drenched with sweat as he ploughed his way across the mountain, trying to control his turns, mastering the speed and gradient of the slope. He never admitted to being tired or asked to stop for a break. So we would plan stops and rests when his falls became more frequent and heavy.

There wasn't an abundance of snow that year, so many of the slopes had grassy, icy or rocky patches and we winced when we saw him fall. Each fall, always on the same side, was followed by loud swearing. One such fall left him with the most impressive bruise from his left hip to the middle of his thigh, a raspberry-blackcurrant swirl of a bruise that made him flinch if we accidentally touched him, so another hard fall onto rocks or ice justified the loud cursing that reverberated across the mountain. It was, at least, one way of locating him easily among all the other skiers on the slope.

Otherwise, looking out across the mountain to the many skiers coming down, Ben didn't stand out as different from the rest. He didn't have a particular style that set him apart from anyone else. As he pushed himself with the challenge of managing more and more difficult slopes, we covered several ranges and valleys in a day, thrilling us even more than it thrilled him, I think. It seemed he had a residual memory of how he used to ski and was determined to get closer to that before the ski trip was over.

However, it was just as well we were there to guide him down, placing ourselves at route crossing points to make sure he took the right way. He admitted he hadn't a clue where he was or how to get from one slope to another, and mostly couldn't tell one lift from the next as they all looked the same to him. He focused on the immediate slope, the next bump or turn, but couldn't internalise the bigger map. To be honest, not all of us can. But he recognised he would be completely lost without someone to show him the way.

We all agreed the trip had been a resounding success and beyond everybody's wildest expectations. It would never have occurred to us even to suggest he come skiing with us. Yet again, the advice from Dr Valenzuela back in the Dominican Republic all those months ago, to 'follow the patient', was spot on.

We returned to the resort the following year as a family, with Miles joining us as well. A year had gone by and Ben made further progress. He was now able to ski with Miles and Theo, both accomplished skiers, sometimes setting off early before the rest of us went out. Still as determined, and much more organised than he had been last time, it felt as though he was more part of the group, without the need for us to plan for him and accommodate his needs. That year there was loads of snow, so any fall led to a softer landing – no whopping bruises and thus no loud expletives ringing out across the mountains.

Ben

But there was more to life than skiing. After the initial disappointment with my work placement, I took a step back to focus on other skills I could improve. In fact, I spent a lot of time taking driving lessons. I'd been lucky enough to get some money from Social Services to support my recovery. I could spend it as I liked, so long as I could account for where it went. This was very helpful because it enabled me to employ Andrew and pay for him to come to Glastonbury with me. I was also able to pay for Alex in the gym and for Ali to help sort my co-ordination out through Tai Chi. I've benefited from all of this immensely. I'm so grateful that, because of this system, I was able to come up with the perfect combination of support. So having this money allowed me to choose how to continue my recovery and I decided I had to get my driving up to speed.

So, oddly, after having been knocked down by a car, I was now learning to drive again, having already got my licence once. The bizarre thing was, I was completely confident I knew how to drive. I'd get behind the wheel and think, *I know how to do this.* Just as I used to jump into a swimming pool thinking I knew how to swim, I'd just go for it – I went ahead on roundabouts and at junctions, where you have to wait until it is clear, thinking it would be fine if I just nipped in there. Thankfully, my driving instructor had dual controls so he could apply the brakes when I was accelerating at the wrong time. Having been a very timid driver before the accident, I was now fearless and downright dangerous. It is quite ironic that after surviving the consequences of reckless driving, I was driving almost as recklessly myself.

This was the last bit of driving tuition I squeezed in before giving up, and it's a great thing I did because I have gone from thinking *It's fine* to realising when it is dangerous. It is funny, though, because I don't think I have ever driven as much before.

At Easter 2013, about six months after I'd finished my master's, I went to visit my friend Jezard who was living and working in Hong Kong. It was a kind of reverse exchange visit: Jezard had come with Miles to visit me when I was living and working in southern Thailand for the third year of my BSc at Bath.

I had an excellent year in Thailand. It had taught me a lot about myself and how to deal with serious difficulties. The devastating Boxing Day tsunami had hit while I was holidaying in Cambodia. On my return to work, near the east coast, I was all too aware of the disaster that had struck the western shore and so many other countries. It was a testing time but I got through it.

But this time, I was the one going to see Jezard in a far-off land, rather than the other way around. It was also an exotic, faraway place that made me feel as though I was really exploring again, as I used to do before the accident.

The first few days were spent in Hong Kong, where Jezard is based, and it really felt like a different Asian city. It had many qualities I was used to, bringing back memories from when I lived in south-east Asia. The pace of life, and the food, brought back specific memories buried deep in my mind. I was very happy for them to resurface. My trip to Hong Kong gave me a renewed sense of the organised chaos that characterises such cities.

I had a weekend to get to see Hong Kong, meet Jezard's friends and discover a bit about his life there. Oddly, Hong Kong also still felt very much like an English outpost. Jezard's life seemed like something left over from the Empire. He earns a huge amount of money with very little or no tax and has a lot of British friends, most of whom are characters we met at university.

For some variety, we decided to get out of Hong Kong, which gave my trip a more adventurous slant. We took a plane to Taipei, an hour's flight from Hong Kong, for five days based in Taiwan. Taiwan was quite different from Hong Kong, not as fast-paced or high-powered. Life didn't seem as hectic and we also had more time there to relax. There was plenty of time to spend getting around and there was less going on in comparison to Hong Kong, where I'd been swept up into my friend's life and the extra distraction it brought.

Jezard knew Hong Kong very well and this was the great perk of spending a few days with him there first – for instance, he'd taken me to some back-street dim sum bar where we'd eaten like kings for very reasonable prices. However, neither of us had been to Taiwan before so we were unprepared for its delights. I did have one guide book, the only one between us, to get some ideas of things to do and places to explore, but going with Jezard was a good move as he was familiar with life in Asian cities and what to look out for.

For one thing, he was keen for us to get a full body massage before we left Taipei. So one day we set out to find one. We'd talked about it as we had lunch and joked about how these things could get interesting if they turned out to be sexy full body massages where you might be massaged by beautiful young ladies.

However, the massage parlour we went to seemed like one of the typical everyday massage parlours around the town. We were told to undress and get into some shorts left for us to change into. As we were waiting to see who our masseuses would be, we were told to lie face down on two massage beds which each had a hole big enough for you to put your head in, looking straight down at the floor. So when the masseuses came in I couldn't see them; I could only see their feet walking about. When someone began massaging me, I was wondering who they were and thinking our masseuses could be two gorgeous women.

As it happened, there wasn't much time for me to think about it because the massage I received was certainly not a relaxing one. It was quite intense, with a lot of slapping and hard pummelling, to the point where I thought it was neither nice nor enjoyable. The most difficult bit was when they pulled my arms back to contort my body into shapes that made me breathe out violently as if I had been winded. So, to be honest, this wasn't a relaxing, sensual body massage but full of pain and discomfort.

When the masseuses had finally finished they said, 'Thank you, that is it.' To my surprise and disappointment, the voices were of two middle-aged Taiwanese men. That certainly sent any ideas of sexual pleasure flying out of the window.

Nevertheless, the whole trip was a great re-introduction to travelling to a place that was very different to the UK and it gave me the excitement of exploring somewhere with a different culture, language and lifestyle.

Rediscovering this excitement reminded me why I enjoyed travel so much and why I worked in my chosen field. The trip was full of examples of the different ways of being and the different values everyone has. It made me feel hugely excited at the prospect of working in international development again.

Andrew

As it turns out, I did decide to move to Barcelona with Guillermo and we left Brighton in late February 2012. Ben attended my farewell party at the Fiddler's Elbow, which was a funny affair as it also happened to be pub quiz night so we entered with a rather large team – and we won! The winnings were just enough to cover 20 shots to share between everyone.

The next time I saw Ben was when he came to visit for a long weekend in February 2013. It had been almost a year since we'd last seen each other and we were both excited to catch up.

Ben had last been to Barcelona just before he started his master's course at Sussex. He'd flown out to see an old friend or, as he put it then, 'to get lucky'.

'Well how was it?' I'd asked when we met for lunch after he'd got back.

'Barcelona was great,' he answered. 'It's surprising how much of it I remembered from being there before.'

'And?'

'And what?'

'And your friend?'

'Ah. She was as I remembered her – very sweet and, amazingly, still single.' He stopped right there.

'And...?' I asked, perking up.

'Oh yes, that too,' he said, looking at me with a huge grin.

Later, he became a little upset with this woman. She'd gone and got herself a Portuguese boyfriend and a little bit of drama ensued. By the time he'd come to Barcelona again, he was no longer friends with her.

I met Ben at Plaça de Catalunya after his bus ride from the airport. It struck me how much he'd changed. His posture, his walk, and his demeanour were all better and his shaking had very much diminished. He also spoke more clearly and less nasally. He'd become very nasal-sounding after his accident as the brain injury and facial trauma had affected his sinuses, which normally add resonance and clarity to the voice. The doctors had told him this would improve in time and they were right, for once. He looked relaxed and happy, and rather quietly confident.

'Here – a present,' he said after we arrived at my apartment, handing over what at first appeared to be a box of massive chocolate fingers.

'I know that smell. Are these cigars?'

'I've had them for ages, but haven't had a chance to smoke them yet. They're yours now,' he said, rather pleased.

'Um, thanks,' I replied, bemused.

That night, Guillermo and I took Ben out to a local tapas restaurant and we stuffed our faces with Catalan specialities. Back at the apartment we cracked open a bottle of our finest to celebrate the reunion while catching up and reminiscing. At some point, Ben thought it would be a good idea to open the box of cigars and light up. Guillermo soon snuck off to bed. He was working the next day but luckily I had taken the day off. I say 'luckily' because shortly into our second or third (I wasn't counting) bottle of vino, I started to feel a little queasy. The nicotine-infused air wafting around wasn't helping, either. Luckily, Ben wanted to go to bed at this point, which was about three or four in the morning. No sooner had we said goodnight, my stomach and head started churning and spinning in an altogether horrific contradiction. Before I knew it, I was hovering over the toilet bowl, half listening to Ben in the dim distance laughing and shouting, 'Andrew, is that you being sick?'

The next day was rather torturous, at least for me. Ben seemed completely fine.

'I can't believe you smoked the cigars last night,' Guillermo said over a stupidly early breakfast.

'That is definitely what made me sick,' I mumbled.

Ben laughed and called me a lightweight.

That morning Ben and I visited the Picasso Museum and later went to La Boqueria market for lunch. That evening we took it fairly easy (easy as in we didn't smoke any cigars) but stayed up nattering till God-knows-what-time. Ben had lots to tell us about his master's, the stupid lectures, his job prospects or the lack of them. He certainly didn't seem to get as tired as he used to, nor did he get as inebriated as before. As a matter of fact, he seemed rather accustomed to it all.

Saturday was overcast and the three of us skipped a planned walk around the city and went instead to the Fundació Joan Miró Art Gallery. In the afternoon, we met some of my friends for a coffee and again that evening for tapas and drinks around the Gràcia area of the city. Ben was in flying form the entire day and chatted easily to people he'd just met for the first time. That night our friend Antonio came round to the apartment and we listened to some music I'd recently composed on my computer. Ben was quite impressed.

'I was half expecting you to say, "It's a bit shit",' I told him. We all laughed. He'd given up that sentence, it seemed.

The next day, Ben was due to fly back around 3pm. This gave us enough time to have a good breakfast, see Gaudí's Sagrada Familia and then take a leisurely walk to Plaça de Catalunya so Ben could catch a bus to the airport. On the way, Guillermo and I decided Ben needed to try *churros con chocolate* (a type of Spanish doughnut stick served with hot chocolate) before he left Barcelona. We took him to a lovely authentic churro place run by a very old Catalan couple who had been in the business, it seemed, since Picasso and Miró themselves had walked the city.

Now, whatever had happened to the pair that morning (mislaid their glasses, perhaps), they seemed to have got it all completely wrong. In fact, they'd committed the cardinal sin of baking: mixing up the salt and sugar. Ben didn't mind at all, or at least didn't seem to notice the churros tasted like monkey's arse. Disgusted, Guillermo and I threw ours, half-eaten, in the bin. We arrived at Plaça de Catalunya just in time for Ben to catch the midday bus, said our goodbyes and promised to catch up soon. And, just like that, the bus and Ben were gone.

That afternoon, I was hovering over the toilet bowl – again. I couldn't help but chuckle, imagining Ben rapidly moving towards the aeroplane toilet in quiet, frenzied desperation. He never said anything when we spoke later. Unsurprisingly, we haven't been back to the famous churros place since.

Hugh

It is said brain damage often leads to changes in personality, particularly when there is damage to the frontal lobes of the brain, which are involved in controlling our desires and impulses. This has been the case with Ben. He has become much more short-tempered and less tolerant than before. Having spent more time with him than anyone else has, and being closely involved in helping him recover, I have often been the target of this. I think his underlying personality is much the same, it's just that instead of muttering under his breath he now comes straight out with whatever his negative thoughts are at the time. His brother and sister, who see him relatively infrequently, have found this very difficult to cope with. I know why he reacts like this so I find it easier to let it pass over me. We do, mostly, correct him, and tell him his reaction is unnecessary, and just occasionally I've bitten back, which has usually resulted in him showing remorse.

What is encouraging is that we can see he is beginning to control these impulses. Sometimes we can see the bile rising but then he checks it and makes his point in a reasoned way instead of just being offensive. His friends have never said anything about him being directly offensive to them. If he has been, they've remained unswervingly loyal and his friendships have been sustained. We'll never know if this is a result of the constant feedback he's had from us about his behaviour or if it would have happened naturally.

However, we often wonder how things might have turned out without the huge support we've given Ben. If he'd had no immediate family to support him, no extensive network of friends, things would undoubtedly be very different. A 2013 study carried out on behalf of the Disabilities Trust Foundation found that 47 percent of a sample of male offenders in the prison system had suffered a serious head injury and three-quarters of these had suffered the injury before committing their first offence, suggesting a causal relationship. Very similar figures have also been reported for rough sleepers.

Jenny and I have the same hopes for Ben's future as any other parents. We want him to have a happy and productive life, in a stable relationship, with a fulfilling career. That is by no means impossible for him but it's less likely than it was before. As a family, our outlook and understanding of the fragility of our lives on this planet have been forever changed. I will never forget the desperate helplessness I felt when walking at a snail's pace behind Claudio, our helper and guide in Dario Contreras hospital, to the pharmacy a few hundred yards from the hospital entrance to buy essential drugs for Ben that the hospital could not provide, and the elation I felt back in the UK when Ben took his first steps down the hospital corridor. Neither will I ignore a rough sleeper again.

Traumatic brain injury (TBI) is much more common than we think. It is estimated that around 1 million people in the UK live with its effects. Recent high-profile cases include the snowboarder Kevin Pearce, about whom the documentary film *The Crash Reel* was released in 2013, and both Michael Schumacher and Jules Bianchi from Formula One motor racing. We all need a greater awareness of the dangers and consequences of TBI.

Despite the publicity that apparent scientific breakthroughs get, psychologists and neurologists still have only a very superficial understanding of how our brains work, how we store memories, and how we can so successfully perceive and act on our environment. Neural imaging, around which there has been so much media hype in recent years, is a very crude way of looking at the workings of the brain. Simply identifying which areas are active during particular tasks tells us next to nothing about how these processes take place and they remain little understood.

Until a very few years ago it had always been claimed that we are born with a finite number of brain cells and once these are lost there is no way back. We now know that, deep within our brains, neurons regenerate continually throughout our lives, although where they migrate within the brain, and their impact on functioning, is still something of a mystery. Very recently, doctors have taken the first steps towards re-joining spinal cord nerves through the implantation of nerve cells taken from the nose. Findings such as these, along with Ben's positive attitude and his undoubted determination to succeed, give us hope and encouragement for his continuing recovery.

Christmas dinner with extended family in Devon, December 2013

Jenny

Some aspects of Ben's recovery are quirkier than others. We don't always know where the changes come from! These are some of the more peculiar aspects of Ben's transformation:

- He has a very sweet tooth. We've been told this is a brain-injury thing. Before his accident, Ben rarely opted for ice cream or chocolate, he left sweets untouched and never seemed tempted by anything sweet or sugary. Well, now these are a definite preference and sometimes a daily choice, which he makes the extra effort to get from the local shop.
- His preference for the colour red. He's comfortable in red. It's become a bit of a family joke. If it's red, we know he'll like it!

- Judging volumes. If there's a choice of size when it comes to pouring a drink or helping himself to food, Ben will always choose the biggest around – the biggest bowl, portion or quantity. He will cook twice as much as he needs or help himself to as much as his plate or bowl will accommodate.
- Saying 'no'. We love it when he says no – this is really rare. He usually says 'yes' automatically to offers of drink or food. However, the 'yes' thing also means he's always a willing participant, up for just about anything. This continues to amaze us.

Accepting the Past

In the few short times I'd met Jazz, she seemed so open, honest and strong. She could handle herself among the close-knit Brighton friends, and that wasn't an easy feat for a new person on the scene. Warm and big-hearted, I could see she made Ben very happy. They had big plans.
Caspar Chater, a friend since childhood

*

Ben

After the accident, I couldn't remember anything about Jazz for two years. I had to focus on getting better and had my time taken up with getting back into shape physically and going back to university.

All through that time I relied very much on what my friends remembered of Jazz. Their memories were a way of making up for the memories I didn't have. But then, two years after the accident, some memories suddenly came back. I specifically remembered the tattoos she had, and her voice. I could distinctly remember her Canadian accent. At the same time, I remembered the name 'Max', although I didn't know where this came from. I emailed Kalinda, Jazz's friend who I'd met in Haiti, and told her that memories of Jazz were coming back. I also wrote, 'I remember the name Max. Do you know who that is?'

Her response was simple: 'Max is my husband and you met him the week your accident took place.' This was extremely encouraging, as it showed my memory can still come back, even though this was never a given but a questionable possibility from the number of doctors I asked about this.

Although I now have some recollection of Jazz, including some general aspects of her personality, my memory is fractured and I don't really have a distinct memory of how I felt about her. I'm sure this is a blessing in disguise, as I have escaped some of the pain of grief.

Perhaps this delay in my memory coming back helped me to focus on staying fit and regaining my skills. It allowed me not to dwell on the accident and grieve over the fact Jazz wasn't there anymore. I had to focus on my life as it was now and maximise my potential. But I'm glad I can now remember something about her, at last.

Jenny

Originally we'd been told not to mention Jazz or her death until Ben brought her up himself. But he didn't. We were all apprehensive about the dreaded question – how to tell him, how to manage his reaction. But things don't usually turn out the way you think they might, so the first conversation went a bit like this: 'So how many girlfriends have I had?' 'Well, about four that we know of.' And then no follow-up.

When his sister was next home they scrolled through some old photos on his computer, stopping to share names and guessing where they'd been taken, as many over the past few years were from Ben's time working abroad. Then a picture of Jazz flashed up on the screen and straight away Ben asked who it was; he commented on how lovely she looked and asked how he knew her. Naomi told him but there was no emotional response as he couldn't remember her at all.

To help him remember, we looked on his phone and found a short piece of video of him and Jazz laughing together in bed. It was hard for us to listen to this short clip: Jazz's voice ringing out, memories of her flooding back. Friends sent in photographs of Ben and Jazz at a friend's wedding, Jazz's mum sent a video of Jazz at a family event – but none of this was sufficient to unlock his memories of her.

Now that Ben was aware of Jazz's death in the accident, it was no longer an unmentionable subject and friends who knew them both started bringing photos of her when they came to visit. Ben also asked about her, their relationship and what their future might have held. So there was Ben: honest, direct and without the memory to support any emotional response. Friends sometimes found this difficult. They weren't always best placed to answer his questions, didn't necessarily share a common point of view and, in some cases, had a stronger sense of grief.

It became the consistent question he asked specialists: when would his memory of Jazz come back? They explained that two years after the accident was sufficient to say with certainty he wouldn't remember if he hadn't already. It was always difficult for them to say this to him and I was touched by their regret and empathy in expressing this certainty for his future, which they were helpless to do anything about. Ben always seemed resigned and soon stopped asking, accepting that was the way it was.

When Jazz's mother and sister each came to England from Canada to visit family, they also came to see Ben and we thought that might be the trigger. Their voices and mannerisms were so like Jazz's, and her sister's likeness so striking, we felt that if meeting them hadn't helped him reconnect with that part of his life then he really wouldn't ever remember her. These visits didn't provide the expected trigger for Ben.

Some time after logging on to his old computer for the first time, he came across some academic files Jazz and he must have worked on together. (The sight of Ben and Jazz at their computers, at the kitchen table or sitting on the sofa together, getting their coursework done for their LSE master's is, for me, an abiding memory of them from when they came to stay.) Something about this process, Ben's accessing old study files, must have triggered something that finally reconnected to her in some way: his memory was difficult to put into words but it included the tattoo on her leg. He can't place much else about her but he has the satisfaction that there is something of Jazz he does remember.

Miles

When Ben's family rushed overseas to take care of him after the accident, I remained one of the links in the chain of communication in the UK. Because they were so far away and I was just hearing second-hand reports, it all felt quite unreal. I'm someone for whom news like that doesn't really sink in until I see evidence and I think in a way that is still true of Jazz's death. Because she'd been away for a while, and because I never went to the funeral, it often just feels as though she's still simply 'away'. I see her constantly in other people, on the tube or in the street.

I think that feeling of unreality I've experienced myself has only been heightened by the way Ben's brain has blocked Jazz out of his memory in such an astonishingly precise manner.

I feel that this, and the fact that Ben didn't remember her, meant she kind of got lost in the whole saga. I'm sure she'd understand that because of how things panned out, all our attention was centred on Ben's staying alive and his subsequent recovery.

Naomi

And then there's Jazz. I don't see Jazz out and about, like Miles does. He still 'sees' her on the tube or in the pub, but I can close my eyes and remember the details of her so vividly, like she's standing in front of me. The grey hairs around her hairline. Her laugh and the way her left eye used to almost squint when she laughed hard.

When Ben was still in hospital I dreamed about Jazz. She was shaking me to wake me up. She wanted to know where Ben was and if he was okay. She was sitting on a chair in the corner of my room. I told her where he was and that he was going to be okay. She called him Monkey. I remember waking up, freezing, and turning the lights on because I was convinced she was there.

We waited for a long time for Ben to ask about Jazz. We were waiting to grieve with him. But he didn't ask. He just asked whether he'd had a girlfriend. When I took him through photos of Jazz for the first time, he was completely blank. Those pictures didn't mean anything to him.

Travelling the world for work, from Mongolia to Africa and to the Carribean, made Jazz a bit of a nomad in my eyes and it meant she had friends all over the world, but friends in London were all waiting to share the grieving experience with Ben when he remembered. We all thought the time would come to grieve for her and remember her, but it never did. We've never had that opportunity.

At the beginning, I thought a lot about Jazz's family and how hard it must have been and how it must have been made harder by Ben seemingly having no recollection of her at all. Ben almost seemed to become frustrated by it and now rarely talks or asks about her. I think he felt a weight at the beginning – why did she die and he survive? Why couldn't he remember? It's amazing what the brain can do in aid of self-preservation. I'm not sure Ben will remember more about Jazz now, even if his brain wanted him to.

David, a friend of Ben's and Jazz's from LSE

As I write this, it's been almost six years since I met Ben and Jazz. Fully remembering the innumerable conversations, shared moments, feelings and perceptions is an impossible task and much has inevitably been lost to time. I've started, deleted and rewritten this short testament on and off over many months, now becoming years, trying to truthfully capture my recollections and not do a disservice to Jazz's memory and Ben's experiences.

I think I met Jazz in the fourth-floor café in the Old Building at LSE – at least, this is my earliest memory of her. She'd evidently already met Ben because she and the group I was hanging out with, and myself by extension, were discussing her infatuation for him and her determination to make him hers. For a 22-year-old guy, new to London and feeling unsettled by the whole experience, this confidence was an intimidating characteristic in a woman. I remember her pierced nose (I later saw her pierced tongue as well), stylish bulky skater shoes, thick North American accent and seemingly constant smoking – features that somehow both complemented and contrasted with her natural beauty. My first impressions were that she was engaging, interested and, simply, cool.

I don't think I'd met Ben at this point, and can't actually remember the first time we did meet. This doesn't reflect well on my memory, but the fact I just seem to remember us being friends represents him well. I remember no introductions or early conversations, no time spent getting the measure of each other, just him simply being a mate. At some point we must have realised we were both from Brighton and had links through family and friends, and sharing this naturally made us seem closer. My early perceptions of Ben were similar to those I had of Jazz, but replacing any potentially intimidating characteristics with a general laid-back-ness, which makes your average almost-hippie Brightonian seem uptight. With Ben being a couple of years older than I was, having more experience in 'the sector' (the currency of respect at the time) and being confident in his critiques of our professors, I looked up to him.

Having set her sights on Ben, Jazz evidently did a good job of getting what she wanted – though I'm sure Ben wasn't complaining. My defining image of their courtship – of which I have only vague recollections – involves them huddled up in winter clothes outside the George IV, each with a pint in one hand and a cigarette in the other. As a couple their spirits naturally matched. They were both up for partying when others would go to bed; for chatting endlessly about friends – both were good listeners and careful observers.

Ben and Jazz, 2009

Looking back over past emails and messages from Ben, I found they concerned pretty much only two things, the first of which was helping me find opportunities. To me and to many others, Ben played the role of life advisor, a role he shared with Jazz. This involved being somewhere between a life coach and strategy consultant, helping me work out what I wanted in life, making suggestions, giving ideas and trying to help me get there. With a natural warmth and generosity, he would pass on contacts, review my amateurish CVs and forward posts about work or internships.

Jazz gave me plenty of this kind of support too, but she also took on the unenviable task of talking frankly about emotions, aspirations and desires with a young Englishman. She approached it with much gusto, though few successes. She had a listening ear and a knowing glance, and offered well-considered and ambitious advice.

The second thing those old email messages concerned was meeting up to, well... drink. I have many memories of pints around campus and exploring nearby pubs for a cheap ale; of Ben's distinctive stuttered throaty laugh as he leaned back slightly, all the while critiquing the world of development and academics, confident something wasn't right and looking around intellectually for things to blame.

Both Ben and Jazz were independent and ambitious. They had an integrity that led them to want to do something worthwhile rather than something simply conferring status. Looking back, I have the strong sense that what I interpreted at the time as Ben knowing what he was doing was really a mixture of confidence and excitement, a willingness to take risks where others would shy away. He took on life with an ease that was foolhardy, adventurous and brilliant, and his canal-boat lifestyle was a great example of this. This brings to mind so many good memories – sipping wine wearing mittens against the cold, eating his homemade soup, drinking tea on the roof in better weather, revising development management in Islington – as well as the more mundane, such as trudging along to a petrol station on a freezing day to fill up the boat's petrol canisters.

Part of me suspects the boat served as a convenient excuse to sleep at Jazz's in these cold, early-winter days. But, close as they were, their strong and similar personalities also grated. Their independence and personal drive would push them to different countries, to argue, to be unsure where life was taking them or where they wanted it to take them. Their mutual stubbornness and forthrightness would lead to arguments and rumblings of tension I sensed only from time to time. As a couple they weren't perfect.

After the course, Ben took up opportunities in Kenya with Oxfam and in Germany with Transparency International. Opportunities just seemed to find him, though in truth his success was down to his careful navigation of the professional world. Jazz had less luck and spent months applying for positions, bank bills rising all the time. She was in a difficult situation and unsure where life would lead. She flat-hopped around London, spending a couple of months on and off in our tiny spare room in Brixton, laptop by her side, searching for jobs, going out for a quick smoke, eating as cheaply as possible and walking about the market.

For Jazz, the position in Haiti was an exciting prospect though she was unsure whether she wanted to work in emergency contexts. I don't remember clearly the last time I saw her, though I vaguely recollect saying goodbye around the Victoria Station area, perhaps even taking a photo outside Westminster Cathedral. Another memory lost to time.

I found out about the accident through a Facebook message from a mutual LSE friend, Kalinda, who'd been close to Jazz out in Haiti. It was early afternoon. I was sitting in my flat in Brixton, the one Jazz had spent a couple of months in and where Ben had hung out regularly. As soon as I began to grasp the meaning of the message I panicked and felt sick, as I'm sure everyone else did in those moments before fully comprehending. I scanned the message desperately, trying to understand, all the while my mind racing and tears creeping in. The enormous sense of loss, desperation, anger and fear was overwhelming, but undoubtedly nothing compared to that felt by both Jazz's and Ben's families.

Not knowing what to do, I immediately called mutual friends. Looking back, I wish I'd been more tactful. Out of desperation, I blurted out to Robbie and Campbell what had happened in a haze of emotion. Both of them, in true Ben-and-Jazz fashion, were enjoying the afternoon in the pub. Those friends still in London – Anna, Laka, Robbie and Campbell – came down to Brixton. We spent the day in tears, staring at the ground and walls in disbelief. We all shared the same feelings: pain, dizziness, anguish, an angry sadness.

It's impossible to summarise Jazz, to put her into a box with neat categories. She, like anyone, was different with different people. Jazz to me was someone I looked to – I looked to her for advice, I called her to have a cheeky pint, to ask for a recipe, to natter. She was fun, she was passionate, insecure, inquisitive, opinionated, adventurous, caring, considerate, beautiful, cool. The way her life ended was disgusting and absurd. I will always remember her knowing glance and be inspired by her adventurous drive and forthrightness.

Aoife, a friend of Jazz's from LSE

It was early on in the academic year, and all the students in the development department at LSE were invited to a 'get to know each other' party at the Quad nightclub on Houghton Street. The music finished up pretty early so a small group of us found our way to O'Neill's bar in Covent Garden. I'd opted to do a combination of anthropology and development and was struggling to get my head around the opposing approaches of the two disciplines. I got talking to a girl from Canada who'd studied anthropology for her undergraduate degree. She was outspoken but measured, sassy and gorgeous. She recounted stories from Mongolia, was scathing about VSO (Voluntary Service Overseas) and assured me I would 'get' anthropology in no time. Her name was Jazz.

She introduced me to Ben, who was a student on the development management course. I was impressed. While I'd been completely absorbed by a nerdy obsession with choosing between courses and attending all my lectures, this girl had fitted in the flirting and getting-together with a guy on our course! She confided she'd spotted him on one of the first days, when he strolled into a lecture hall. 'It was his blue eyes. Don't you think they're amazing?' I'd never talked to Ben and hadn't noticed him strolling into any lecture hall but when he started chatting to me I had to agree: his eyes were magnificent.

Ben and Jazz were easily the coolest couple on our course. Ben lived on a boat, Jazz smoked rollies. While others fretted over essays and courses, they walked in a leisurely way around the LSE backstreets. Jazz had an opinion on everything and I loved bumping into her and getting her take on different lecturers, LSE and life in London. She usually had a story or two to tell about herself and Ben. Jazz adored him and I mainly got to know him through her stories.

In early 2010, I invited Jazz up to Hampstead Heath to fly a kite. We hung out in her apartment afterwards. Ben was in Berlin at the time and she was sharing a flat with his friend Miles. She cooked me up a bean dish, we drank a beer and talked about our year at LSE and our plans for the future. As a grand finale to our time together, she played me a song by Fannypack called *Cameltoe*. We laughed. It was classic Jazz humour.

Jazz's death was the first death of a friend I found out about on Facebook. It was devastating to realise what had happened and to be so far from people who knew her. I'd moved to Bristol and was living with people who'd never known her.

In my effort to come to terms with her death, I found myself endlessly scrolling through her photos on Facebook. As each happy picture appeared on my screen, I wallowed deeper and deeper in a heavy sadness.

As an Irish person, I usually experience an unexpected warmth at wakes and funerals. The mood at these events can careen from sad to comical and, at times, absurd, as people relate stories from different stages of a person's life, usually with the dead person's body within sight. I wasn't able to go to Jazz's funeral as it was so far away. Our friendship seemed so transient and intangible.

I still find it strange when Facebook reminds me it's Jazz's birthday. In the altered reality of the internet, she could very easily still be alive.

Ross, a friend of Jazz's from LSE and a fellow Canadian

I remember it was the second day of autumn in 2010. The early-morning air was cool as I walked through Parc Angrignon in Montréal. The path wound through the trees, leading from the metro station to the far end of the park. From there it was just a short walk to the funeral home where Jazz's family and friends were gathering. Jazz had told me she was planning to come home that fall for a visit, but I never thought it would be like this.

All those little issues in life that seem like a big deal faded away to insignificance in light of what had happened. Hearing about the accident had left me feeling utterly empty. I'd started to wonder whether it would have been better never to have become close to her, to save myself the pain now. It was a horrible thought to have, but attending the funeral of my best friend was a position I never thought I'd be in.

Walking through the park allowed me to reflect on my time with Jazz. I noticed a young child run from his parents in order to chase a flock of birds. His mother followed, chastising the boy for running off. It made me think of Jazz's sense of adventure and her desire to explore new places. Whether it was Mongolia, Uganda, Haiti or London, she was always up for something new and something challenging. Whatever the situation, she could find something unique to admire.

Jazz was the kind of person who knew what she wanted and dedicated herself to succeeding. I was always struck by her resilience and her ability to overcome what seemed like insurmountable challenges. When she fell ill during our master's programme, she missed two months of classes – almost an entire term of a two-term course. Even those who knew of Jazz's tenacity thought taking time off to recover, then continuing at a later date, was the only option. But she wouldn't be persuaded; she'd simply come too far to delay her goal. With dedicated study she not only caught up but excelled in the programme.

After the funeral, friends and family gathered at her mom's house for dinner and to share stories about Jazz. It was clear she'd had the same effect on others as she'd had on me. She was incredibly genuine and sincere in everything she did, even if it meant telling you a truth you didn't necessarily want to hear. Because of this, and her life experience and wisdom, she was my go-to person whenever I needed advice. No matter how intractable my problem seemed to be, she could effortlessly cut to the heart of the issue and make sense of things. She was incredibly caring towards her friends and revelled in their successes while empathising with their pains. I remember the genuine happiness and excitement she felt when I got my first job after grad school, even though she was still looking for work herself.

The day after the funeral, I went down to Montréal's old city. Along the narrow cobbled streets and through the old port, the historic city comes to life. The buildings and roads existed long before me – a stark contrast to our fleeting existence – but this made me realise it is through our actions and our interactions with others that our true legacy is felt and lives on. Jazz's desire to do whatever she could to make the world a better place was clear in everything she did. Her ability to do this directly was cut short just as she was putting her passion and knowledge into practice, but her work continues through those she affected. She always encouraged me to strive for my best and to have fun in the process, and my memories of her always encourage me to work harder. For me, part of accepting what happened means incorporating more of the things I can learn from the way she lived – her love for life, her courage, the way she pursued her goals so intently – into my own life.

As I reflected on all this heading back to Toronto, I knew there could be no substitute for the time we'd shared and the conversations we'd had. People often regret taking a friendship for granted, but I don't have that regret. I knew what kind of friend I'd had in Jazz, how rare and special a person she was, and how lucky I was to have been her close friend.

Kellie, a friend of Jazz's from LSE

My memory of Jazz consists of ridiculously accurate small details: the leggings she used to wear (very tight); the shape of her mouth (perfect); the way she walked (cool and feminine at the same time).

On a Tuesday quite early in the semester, just after we met, we went for a walk around the LSE neighbourhood. I asked her to share her life story, at that time completely clueless that I was in for a real treat. Once Jazz let you into her inner circle, she shared her stories so openly. She took away all the filters. Her emotions were so rich and real.

It took me a long time to figure out what made a friendship with her so special. Contemplating this now, I think I've worked it out. If she was with someone really close to her, she didn't have any shame. *Nada.* She told you what she really thought and what she really felt. No sugar-coating. No twisting. No hiding.

We ended the walk after four hours of detailed life stories: boyfriends, experiments, emotional roller-coasters, her time in Mongolia, the deep relationship with some of her friends, her absolute admiration for her mother (which she struggled to express in a satisfactory way) and so much more. Damn, this young woman had been in situations most of us only read about in books. What I loved most about the way she narrated was how she never portrayed herself as the victim. In some cases, she'd put herself into these situations – seeking excitement, a desire to feel alive.

It's my impression she didn't let many people into her small, trusted circle. When she was with people outside the circle, her shamelessness also fell away. In class, for example, when she was asked to comment, she'd be quite self-conscious. When we stood around with a group of classmates, she'd laugh differently. She was both confident and insecure at the same time. It was a confusing mix. I'm quite sure if you asked ten people who knew her moderately well, they'd all rate her confidence differently. But they'd all agree on one thing. She was unforgettable. Everyone is special and unique, but Jazz was really different. Her dance with life had a different rhythm.

And boy, she had a mission for that life. Well, actually, she had two. First, she wanted to 'give back'. Not because she'd enjoyed privileges and wanted to share them but because she just couldn't stand how ugly the world was. And she had many ideas on how to change that, pit-bull style. Second, she wanted love. Not the type most of us look for; she wanted the real thing. No American-movie-type stuff; real, steamy-hot, deep, all-encompassing love. And she found it in Ben.

I must admit I sometimes felt bad for Ben. Once Jazz showed herself to you, the purity of it all could be overwhelming. It seemed what she had to give in a relationship was endless. It made you fear her lovers would drown in it. This endless love also knocked her off balance sometimes, putting her in a vulnerable, insecure place.

In an email she sent from Haiti, only a few months before the accident, she described a detailed train of thought which illustrates how she loved. The entire email was devoted to this feeling. It went something like this: 'I love my work. The hours are crazy. And sometimes I do not think about Ben. That scares the hell out of me.' She goes on about how she can be so immersed in her work and not think about him. Then, at the end of the email, she reveals the period of time Ben is not on her mind which is causing her so much worry: a few hours. It made me laugh out loud.

Yes, she was good at that. Making people laugh out loud. I would have loved to have witnessed the rest of her dance with life. I miss her.

Liz, a close friend of Jazz's from Canada

Jazz and I met when we were 17 and quickly became friends. Over the years we were many things to one another – roommates, co-workers, party buddies and confidantes. I was her first roommate when she moved out of her mother's home. She visited me when I was in hospital for several months. We encouraged each other to follow our dreams. We comforted each other when things didn't work out as planned.

Jazz was the first friend of mine that my husband, Dave, confided to when he decided he would propose, and she was overjoyed to witness the proposal itself. She came to my wedding, which was held at a roller rink, and donned roller skates even though she'd never skated before. She struggled with life's ups and downs but was always willing to try anything once. By her mid-twenties, Jazz realised her personal struggles could be overcome through helping others. This is what drove her to a career in community development – and into the arms of Ben, who she loved very much.

Our last conversation was over Skype, only a few days before I left for Europe, when she was excitedly waiting for Ben's arrival in Haiti. We told each other to have fun, that we loved each other and we'd speak to each other as soon as we were both back and had a minute to catch up on our adventures.

I was in a hotel in Bayonne, French Basque country, after spending a beautiful day in a nearby coastal town. I had my laptop open and was checking my Facebook. Everything became a slow-motion blur. Kiran, Jazz's sister, had contacted me through Jazz's Facebook. She wrote me a message saying she was sorry to be the one to tell me this, but she had terrible news. Jazz had died in a car accident. I was sitting on the bed but felt like I'd been hurled against the wall behind me. *This had to be a joke! Kiran doesn't know what she's talking about! I just spoke to Jazz, about a week ago! This is a mistake. Maybe she's hurt – but not dead. Right?* I managed to read the email out loud to Dave, who stared back at me, not knowing what to do or how to help. I began to panic. Did I call Kiran first? I didn't know. I felt numb.

I remember calling a mutual good friend of ours, George. He answered without a hello. He just sobbed into the phone and we cried together in silence. I called a few other friends who were in Montréal and could help Kiran and Jazz's mother, Abby, as they tried to figure out exactly what happened. The news I received was second- and third-hand and it never felt like anything made sense. I didn't know what to do with myself. I continued on the next leg of our journey, to Madrid, oscillating between numbness, anger and intense sadness. After I had a panic attack in a museum, I decided I had to get to Montréal as soon as possible. I had to be home, around familiar things and familiar people.

There are many days I imagine having my usual Skype dates with Jazz, when I can talk to her about anything and everything that comes to mind. There is a hole in my life that will never be refilled. As I live my life and achieve various personal and professional goals, not a day goes by I don't catch myself wanting to share these successes with Jazz and hear about hers. I wonder what accomplishments would be under her belt by now, and what her life would have been like. Would she have what she wished for – to have fruitful career experiences and then find a place in the world to settle with Ben? What would she think of the latest fashion trends? How would she wear her hair? How would she age?

Sometimes I meet Jazz in my dreams. We sit next to one another, catching up on these questions. I hug her, if only for a minute, before my consciousness betrays me and I find myself realising this can't happen in real life. I try to pull myself back into the dream a little longer, but it's never the same.

Looking to the Future

*I've wondered to myself what Ben will do with his life. A former employer
suggested he pursue a position in 'disability development',
but that's not something that previously interested him.
I think he doesn't want to be pigeon-holed.*
Roland Susman, a friend since childhood

*

Ben

Throughout my recovery I took big leaps of faith into the unknown because I felt I had to. My attitude was that I simply had to recover, and I stuck to it resolutely. My single goal was to get back to the point where I could go off to somewhere in Africa and work, as I'd been going to do in Rwanda.

My drive has always come from the fact that the accident stopped me doing that. I think if I could get to that stage again, I feel I would have come full circle and it would be a wonderful conclusion to the aftermath of the terrible event that cost Jazz her life. It would give me a huge feeling of achievement.

It has already taken a lot of effort to get to where I am now, facing the difficulties of re-entering the workplace. The problems of getting back into my field have been greater than I thought and I've become a lot tougher about what I'll expect in terms of support as more work has been offered to me.

When I worked for the local international development company, on the climate-change report, I was told I might need to work with people who understood my difficulties and that I should perhaps try looking for work in disability and development. This kind of suggestion angers me to the core. It is completely missing the point. People who say this don't see how I've worked so hard and done another master's. They see my disability as a fixed result of the accident rather than a current stage in the long and active struggle it has been to recover. Still, I'm grateful for that work experience. It was a good placement because it hardened my perception of what I need from employers to allow me to work effectively.

I had another setback the following spring when I worked briefly for a London think-tank on international development. This placement was also given to me through charity, really. It was short-term work and they asked me to do a quantitative analysis assessment of a dataset from a survey in Vietnam using some analytics software that I don't have on my computer and didn't match my skill-set. So it didn't work out. The guy who had given me the job said he'd met somebody who wanted to work in development but found it really hard to get a position and instead decided to be a teacher – implying I should make a similar move. When people tell me I should try something else, it belittles the effort I've put into studying to get back into my chosen field. I can understand my skills didn't match up to expectations and I wasn't necessarily cut out for what the company wanted, but I feel quite strongly I shouldn't have been employed to do these things in the first place if they were unsuitable tasks for me to do.

I did walk away from these two experiences thinking, *What am I not doing right?* As a result, it has made me think about what I can do effectively and try to look for different opportunities to apply for. It's made me realise I need to declare what's happened to me before I go for interview, so people can understand what I've been through. I need to be clear about what I can offer and what I can get back from a work placement.

This is a weak position to be in, though. I've moved away from simply accepting generosity. In looking for employment, I've gone back to people who might give me a chance because they know me, but I always try to judge if an offer is good and people can really use my skills or if it is just a slap on the back and a pointless exercise. I want to know what I'm going to be given to do and why. I want to know the required deliverables and to see how these can be produced.

I was given another chance to work for the think-tank in 2014. I'd applied for the ODI fellowship scheme again and was given an interview that February. It was a tough one. To start with, the head of the programme queried my decision to do governance and development as a master's rather than sticking to economics, which they were recruiting people for. However, I think I answered well by giving some reasons to think about the governance systems in the countries I was applying to help. Unfortunately, the next section of the interview took apart my understanding of economics theory, which had been displaced by the head injury. I was very competent in this before, having done my first degree in economics and international development. Apart from that bit, I thought I answered the questions in the interview well, but they didn't offer me a place. It was a real knock-back and I felt all my efforts to re-train had been disregarded. Still, my contact there offered to see if there was anything else available and in March I was offered some short-term work.

Before working for this organisation again I explained how I wasn't given the right direction before and needed a properly organised task to get on with if I was to be able to fulfil the role required. The person offering the work was confident he could give me the direction I needed. He came up with a clearly defined and do-able task, but then he wanted me to do it within huge time pressures, expecting me to work over the weekend and produce a bibliography by the Monday. This really shows that employers need to give me reasonable allowances when doing a task.

I also had some voluntary work at a tuberculosis charity and, as a last hope of getting into work, I did some work for my dad's company, which focuses on special educational needs. They wanted to learn about how they could apply their model of online training to developing countries, so I did various bits of research for my dad and went with one of his partners to meet UNESCO in Paris. UNESCO passed us on to the Commonwealth of Learning in Vancouver, which seemed to be exactly the sort of organisation Dad's company was looking for and was a great connection for them. So although I was annoyed at being told I should look at other lines of work, perhaps they had a point.

But trying to get back into work has continued to be problematic as I've been unable to find anyone who can give me 'reasonable adjustments'. These are legally binding under the Equality Act 2010, but the organisations I'm interested in all work to very tight timescales, which they cannot compromise with reasonable adjustments. So work with reasonable adjustments is something I've been seeking unsuccessfully for quite a while. When I took part in a drug trial at Hammersmith Hospital they said this was a common problem people faced by people suffering from head injuries.

The difficulty in finding employers willing to offer reasonable adjustments is an ongoing problem. However, I recently had a long chat with someone and we talked about my skills now and discovered I am particularly good at working out the pressures people are under within organisations. Working as a consultant, he often needs someone to work out the dynamics in aid projects he is evaluating, to be a part of his report back to the donors. We will see if this might be the beginning of a role I could play for him in the future.

It is now mid-July 2016 and although I've had one long period of work that has been extremely beneficial to my dad's company by expanding their opportunities for more work, it has not ended in long-term employment. However, I am feeling hopeful that something will come up sooner rather than later. I think it will be good to re-assess my changed skills and think about a wider scope for employment rather than purely development research. With all my efforts and a little bit of luck, I hope I will finally get back into proper employment.

Becky

I met Ben in Berlin. He was an intern where I worked and we began chatting during cigarette breaks. I got to know him better when he was kicked out of his flat (or walked out, after being unreasonably threatened) for not cleaning the bathroom. At first he slept on a friend's floor but after a couple of days he moved into my flat and stayed on the futon in the lounge until he found somewhere else. He was a great house guest. He cooked for us and we spent plenty of time chatting on our balcony late into the evening. I don't think he ever cleaned the bathroom, though!

What I remember most from those conversations, apart from Ben being great company, was that despite his laid-back appearance he was anything but. He was insightful. Although he'd been in Berlin less than a month, he had a clear understanding of the complex issues where we worked. He had strong opinions about work and individuals, and he was determined – when offered an extension to his internship, he declined because of the low pay. On leaving the organisation, he wrote a two-page document about how the treatment of interns could be improved.

By the time Ben left Berlin, we'd become friends. I had a lot of respect for him and was sure he was going on to great success in his life. He was full of the promise of his ODI fellowship in Rwanda and excited to be seeing Jazz soon. Over that summer we kept in touch frequently enough for Ben to pester me about finding another job. And then I stopped getting emails.

I heard about Ben's accident through another intern at work. Her husband had studied with Ben at LSE and she knew he'd been working with us previously. Her information was sketchy. We only knew he'd been in a car accident and was seriously injured, and Jazz hadn't survived.

We were all shocked and upset by the news, but there was very little we could do. We'd only known Ben for a short time, had met Jazz only briefly, and didn't know any of his friends or family. Finally, I found a Facebook page set up by a friend of Ben's to provide information about his progress. It was members-only, but when I requested to join I was able to catch up with the news and at Christmas I sent him a card.

To be honest, I think that would have been it. I would have sent the card and then quietly let it go. I wasn't connected to the family, I didn't want to intrude, and I imagined (correctly) Ben wouldn't even remember me. But his dad wrote back to my old work email address (I had left by then, partly due to Ben's encouragement) and a colleague forwarded it. Hugh encouraged me to visit.

So the next time I was visiting my cousin in Brighton, I saw Ben too. I was really nervous. I wasn't entirely sure why I was there, except I wanted to see how he was doing. Ben was very changed and physically quite frail, more so than I'd expected. He didn't recognise me at the station so I had to introduce myself. We went back to his house and spent the afternoon in the garden with his mother, sister and Miles.

The family were very welcoming and Ben asked me lots of questions, but he didn't remember me. Towards the end of the afternoon he wanted to go to the pub for a drink. This was a bit daunting. I didn't know if he should drink. But over two halves of local bitter I became re-acquainted with the Ben I remembered.

He was angry about the place we'd previously worked at together. Or at least he could remember he was angry, but not what he was angry about. It seemed he was expressing the emotions of a memory without having the full memory itself. We talked about how he'd written the two-page critique of the organisation's intern policy, and he was really proud. I got the impression he was still very curious about himself, trying to work out what kind of person he had been.

Just before he got on the bus home that day, Ben said he was glad I'd come to see him and he could understand from meeting me why we'd been friends before. Apart from this being touching and reassuring for me, a generous gesture on his part, I realised how brave he'd been to meet me in the first place. I'd been nervous about meeting him but at least I could remember who he was. Ben just had my word for it.

So many incidents over the next few years reminded me of the bravery and openness Ben showed in the first years after the accident. He was always open to people, he encouraged them to make contact and was frustrated when they didn't. I think it came from his curiosity about himself, other people and how his life had been before the accident, as well as his great determination to re-build his life in its previous image.

Sometimes Ben's enthusiasm for discovering his past and the people in it proved a disappointment. Some people let him down, or at least this is how he saw it. This occurred in both personal and professional relationships where he found it difficult to understand someone's behaviour or where he felt let down or misled. In the worst cases, he felt discriminated against or that he'd been used in some way. Sometimes I think this was fair. But it's impossible to judge, because Ben could be difficult to communicate with and would get the wrong end of the stick, or have great, but unrealistic and ultimately unfulfilled, expectations.

For the people involved, I'm sure letting Ben down was entirely unintentional and came from a misunderstanding of what he needed or expected, or an over-commitment they couldn't fulfil. But there are also clear cases of discrimination and people's capacity for taking advantage of others or being inconsiderate of their needs. When people or organisations behaved in ways that seemed unfair or unjust, Ben felt this acutely. And it often took him months to come to terms with their behaviour.

When I moved to Brighton in late 2012, Ben was physically well – much fitter than most – and he'd put himself through the mental and intellectual rigours of a master's degree. But he was still unsatisfied, and determined to get back into work and live an independent life.

Just before Christmas 2012, Ben started his first internship following his master's, with an organisation in Brighton. He'd worked with them before the accident and they knew his history, so he had high hopes. He was thrilled to be back at work but, over the next couple of months, it became clear he wasn't getting the support he needed and there were great differences between his expectations and those of the organisation.

The internship ended with Ben being very frustrated and finding it difficult to understand why it hadn't worked out. Frankly, I have to agree his frustration was justified, at least from my perspective, looking on from the outside. Part of the problem seemed to lie with Ben's inability to communicate, or perhaps even recognise, the amount of support he needed from the organisation to fulfil his role. I remember his friends and I always pressed him to ask directly for feedback and guidance, but either he didn't do this or any feedback given wasn't clear enough.

Ben's great motivation came from a desire to return to his previous work in international development. He'd successfully completed his master's and he was in the right place to re-start his career. All he needed was extra support, feedback and clear guidelines. So at the end of the internship he understandably felt frustrated and let down when he was given negative feedback on his performance.

He was also insulted when someone in the organisation, possibly with the best of intentions, advised him he should consider working in 'development and disability'. I still don't fully understand what they meant, despite talking about it a lot with Ben. But Ben took it as an insult and was angry at the implication that people with disabilities should automatically work for a disability organisation rather than follow their true interests. He would have been much better served by an honest assessment of his skills and abilities, and of the areas he needed to improve to achieve his aspirations.

It's a great testament to Ben's determination and strength of character that he didn't give up or lose hope. He has kept applying for jobs, pursued voluntary opportunities to improve his skills, and been successful in getting work elsewhere. He is still not where he wants to be career-wise, but he won't stop trying.

Aoife, a friend of Jazz's from LSE

From the very first time I met Ben after his accident, he was focused on getting back into working in international development. I was really inspired by his determination.

I work for a small development consultancy, which Ben had worked for before the accident. I tried to get him work on upcoming contracts but unfortunately it has been really difficult for him to win consultancy roles. Consultancy in international development is intensely competitive. Graduates from master's programmes are often prepared to work for free or for very little payment, just to gain some experience. Consultancy firms have taken advantage of this and often run poorly paid internship schemes, which graduates compete hard for on the understanding that, to compensate for low pay, they get training in consulting. So interns were picking up the work Ben could otherwise have done to build up his experience again.

In addition, most short-term consultancy contracts in international development are won through open- or limited-competition tenders. Competition forces prices down but the drawback is many of the winning contracts are under-budgeted, with too few days allocated to them. This means there is little time for mentoring on the job or for allowing team members to work at different paces.

So it's not an ideal environment to get Ben back into work. I've been trying to encourage him to consider working for non-governmental organisations (NGOs), an environment where bottom-line incentives are not pushing staff to produce at maximum output all the time and there may be more space for organisations to support and work with him. NGOs may offer more opportunities and be more willing to invest in personnel if they know they'll reap benefits over the longer term.

Ben has been so focused on getting to where he was before the accident that thinking about taking a different direction in his career is almost akin to admitting he can't recover fully. He's not exactly the same as before his accident and different elements of his personality have become stronger. Part of the challenge of writing this book has involved following up wayward contributors such as myself and he has demonstrated a persistence I'm pretty sure he didn't have before his accident.

It's true that Ben is 'Ben' again, but a big part of this recovery journey is about discovering who he will go on to become. That involves letting go of certain aspects of pre-accident Ben and embracing a new version of himself.

Jenny

Anyone bringing up children experiences varying degrees of angst as they grow up, test the boundaries and fly the nest, but having an adult living back home wasn't something we were prepared for, let alone one initially without the wits to look after himself. The anxiety and worry was multiplied manyfold when he went out, putting us through worse than anything we'd experienced when the children made their transitions to adulthood.

When Ben's social horizons first began to broaden, he would be collected by friends and brought back home. The to-ing and fro-ing had a clear beginning and end, which gave us some reassurance. But it wasn't too long before he would be out and meeting friends, usually at the pub, doing the to-ing and fro-ing on his own. Out late, often having had too much to drink, he would come back like a homing pigeon, without us ever knowing how he'd made the journey safely. Torn clothes and bruises would suggest the return had not been straightforward.

Ben's tolerance of alcohol isn't what it used to be and for a time his ability to moderate his intake and say no was totally lacking. At first we weren't used to checking whether his mobile was charged and, when he failed to be home by the early hours, we'd be phoning and getting no answer. Frantic with worry and a rising sense of panic, his siblings would somehow put the word out and manage to track him down. He agreed during those early days to have an app on his phone to locate him when out of the house (if the phone was charged). This gave us some peace of mind.

Not having an 'off-switch' to his alcohol consumption meant that, once home, Ben would seek out any alcohol lurking in cupboards. So the solution was to become an alcohol-free house. We don't have drink at home unless in very small and limited amounts. Over the years, repeated incidents would show he had no long-lasting desire to moderate his drinking behaviour. The only time he managed to maintain a no-drinking period was when doctors recommended it in order to avoid any possibility of seizures, but eventually this restriction was lifted and Ben had the all-clear to drink. The impact of a binge is predictable and telling: deteriorating memory, lack of clarity in his speech and a return to his shakiness, which affects everything he does.

While he sets his own limit, I know this is hard for him to stick to. One particularly severe episode saw his dad and I reach a new level of despair for the first time since those initial days after the accident. He came in legless in the early hours after a long day's drinking, his drunken state signalled by the slamming of the front door and a thump that signalled he was unable to stand. Hugh rushed downstairs to find him on the floor in his own mess, which between us we cleared up in a fit of blind rage – not so much that we were dealing with his shit, his torn and dirty clothes, his grazed hands and elbows, but that this state was repeated every few months, each time confirming to us that he was incapable of managing this aspect of his behaviour. It was blind rage at the state he was in; blind rage at the risk he must have taken in getting himself back home; blind rage at his group of friends who between them must have been aware that as one group left him to another group as the day and evening wore on, someone should have ensured that he stopped drinking. Not easy, I know, but the consequences are not easy either and likely to end badly. We were in despair that all our efforts and his were being pissed away; despair at the realisation that the boozing could be his undoing – his undoing socially, intellectually, and by scuppering all his slim chances of picking up the thinnest of life's threads.

Ben at the time appreciated the impact this was having on us and understood all his progress would amount to nothing if he didn't get his drinking under control. His drinking brings back all the early anxieties that I recognise in my thumping heart, my lack of sleep, my rage, which I direct at him. I weep, shout and thrash about verbally, directing it all at him. I now manage it by telling him that as long as

I still feel like this, I will continue to express my anxiety if he goes out with a certain group of hard-drinking friends. His drinking still makes us very anxious but we know the only person who can do anything about it is Ben. But incidents have remained more dispersed and their regularity less frequent.

I hope we reach a point where this is no longer a source of worry and there's no longer the need for us to remind him of his resolve before he goes out. We also hope Ben can feel part of things socially without drinking to excess. He will always need to keep tight control of his drinking or it will be his undoing. It would have been more helpful had the medics said staying off alcohol altogether was best for him long-term rather than giving an arbitrary consumption figure as 'safe'. I look at homeless people or local drunks and can't help but ask myself, *Have they had a head injury?* Without the ongoing support of a loving family, we feel this could be Ben's path.

Four years on and Ben is more and more independent, and on his way to feeling ready to move away from home. There's nothing we want more for him. He stays home alone for several weeks at a time, the house is in good order when we return, he hasn't wasted away and no disaster has had to be coped with. While I know he appreciates the safety net living at home provides, thankfully he has a strong sense that being at home with Mum and Dad isn't normal. He continues to pursue employment opportunities with great resilience and determination. He's still seeking to make use of his past experience and interests as a means to lead a fulfilling and purposeful life that will bring with it financial security in order to provide himself with the independence he now craves.

We have no doubt Ben will achieve this in time. We hope that his incredible determination and drive remain a feature of his personality and that the world looks kindly on him, cutting him some slack without making too many allowances. If I have one wish, it is that, though he may choose to live and be alone, I wouldn't want him ever to be lonely.

Naomi

I remember, early on, when Ben hadn't been at home long, crying in my kitchen in London with Miles and my best friend Kate. I was crying because Ben wasn't the same Ben and I wasn't sure I liked him. I felt I wasn't allowed to grieve for the old Ben because he was still here. I couldn't let him know I missed the old Ben. I've never let him know that. Kate told me I would learn to love the new Ben, but at the time I so desperately wanted the old Ben. I still miss the old Ben, terribly. But as time goes by, the old Ben fades and the new Ben replaces him. Miles found an old recording of the radio show they used to do at university. When we listened to it, I didn't even recognise Ben's voice. That made me sad.

I want Ben to stop searching for the old Ben. I want him to discover who he is now. That might mean he won't necessarily like the same things as he did before. He needs to know that's okay. I want him to find a passion, whatever it is. He used to be passionate about cooking, and cooking Thai food in particular. But I'm not sure he has any passions now.

I worry he often replaces this void with pointless boozing and he socialises with a group of friends who similarly fill their voids with booze. It's a very slippery slope for Ben. He might not like to admit it, but he's extremely vulnerable. He's always been a drinker but it's so distressing to see him do more damage to his brain and see the physical impact it has on him after a night out. I wish his friends were more understanding. I wish they would look out for him and help him discover the new Ben and not keep searching for the old Ben – because he isn't at the bottom of a pint glass.

Theo once found him passed out at the bottom of the stairs because he'd had friends round and drunk himself to the point of oblivion. Theo was shaken up and furious. When he called and told me, I remember physically shaking on the end of the phone because I was so angry. I was furious with Ben's 'friends'. Theo had found him and thought he was dead. Imagine that feeling after everything we'd already been through. Ben didn't understand, and I'm not sure he even understands now, just how distressing we find it and how much worry it causes for everybody.

I hope Ben will become open-minded, open to suggestions and most of all open to the love of his family. He needs to remember we're only ever trying to help, or to have a bit of fun with him and trying to find his sense of humour again.

What people don't tell you is that when people come round from a coma, they don't wake up and ask where they've been. They might open their eyes, but they aren't conscious. They look empty. In the months that follow, this is replaced by a wild, feral look, which doesn't represent the person you knew before. The recovery is long. Ben will be recovering for the rest of his life, but the improvements will become more subtle as time goes on. He is still making progress –

it just becomes harder to see it now he's made it past so many milestones.

I know some of what I've written will make Ben mad. He'll no doubt get his finger out and wave it at me in a fit of rage, but I couldn't contribute to this book and not be honest. His recovery has been miraculous; he's done so incredibly well. I can't believe all he's achieved when I think back to that moment when Dad said life would never be the same again. But it's also been incredibly difficult for everyone involved, and continues to be.

In the end, we're all working towards the same goal, and that is for Ben to be happy and to find his new path in life. And he will find it, of that I am sure.

Ben

Reading Mum's and Naomi's anxieties concerning my recovery, I can completely understand their fears and hopes for me. It puts into perspective the impact my getting better has had on their views and wishes for me. I also appreciate how difficult this accident has been, not only for me, but for the people around me, too.

I feel the past four years have forced me to re-establish everything about myself, from exploring my drives and motivations again to learning who I actually am. It has been said it takes five years to recover from a head injury and I can say from my own personal experience, it sure does. But writing this book, I can see how far I've come – from traffic accident victim to demon driver; laid-back guy to bossy mate; bedridden wreck to advanced skier; and Andrew's 'patient' to his critical friend.

The one thing that has seen me through this has been my resolve to hold on to my own idea of myself, trying to stick to the motivations and desires I had before. It's helped me achieve incredible things. The master's was a major milestone.

I fully understand Mum's and Naomi's worries when it comes to my drinking, which has been a difficult phase for everyone, including me. It's taken a few years for me to be able to drink responsibly again and leave behind those early days when I couldn't keep control of my alcohol intake or my drunkenness.

Reading Mum's and Naomi's reactions to this emphasises the strains it has placed on everyone in our family. However, I feel quite strongly this was a phase I have passed through and I am now more controlled. I don't get horrendously drunk in the way I used to.

I can understand that Naomi worries about discovering the new Ben, who she might not like as much as the old one. Rediscovering the old Ben has been the journey I've been on for the last four years. It's been difficult, but not without results. I feel I've probably done as much as I can. Yet, in a way, I don't want to leave that journey behind as I feel giving up on it now would be a waste, given the effort involved and the leaps and bounds forward that have been made.

Whatever happens, going through the whole experience of my recovery has put my life into perspective. It has also enabled me to make friends with those who have helped me do things I never would have done otherwise, such as Tai Chi, and to pursue these as best as I could manage.

I feel the uphill struggle I've endured won't necessarily get any easier. There are still more difficulties to overcome but, as time goes on and I continue to make progress, I think my path through life will get smoother and the rough edges of my new self will become more rounded off.

Author's Note

As I want this book to be a testament to the incredible journey I've taken since September 2010, I would like it to be dedicated to the memory of Jazz, the beautiful but elusive girl I couldn't remember for two years. Indeed, I'd been told by doctors those memories were gone and would never come back. I feel my case shows there are several ways the brain can regenerate and that hard work, both physical and mental, can enable you to regain cognitive ability and memories that have disappeared. In this way it's a good example of brain plasticity and perhaps suggests getting away from any Freudian ideas that remembering would be too traumatic, romantic though that idea is. It just took a certain amount of time for those pathways to start to work again – longer than two years.

This book is also dedicated to Jazz's memory because it has necessarily been written in her absence, due to the actions of a young, reckless driver that cost her her life.

Jazz

I would also like to dedicate the production of this book to the kindness of those doctors close to the site of the accident who took it upon themselves to drive me straight to hospital, an act without which I would not even be here to write this account of the trials and tribulations of my recovery. Similarly, I want to pay tribute to the consultant, Dr Valenzuela, who kept me alive in those first weeks and supported my family so well at that dark time. I hope the completion of this book will mark my going on to leave the accident behind me as my life shapes itself anew and goes forward.

My account shows recovery can take place. It is slow and long and in some ways it is continuous. The hurdles you jump are never-ending and continue through time, even though the obstacles become smaller, more manageable and less daunting.

I would like to say thank you to all my friends, who have made it as easy as possible to resume life, as well as a massive thank you to my family, who were on the next plane out to find me. Their determination and dedication have been a tremendous encouragement and have, I think, been matched by my own efforts.

Acknowledgements

This book would never have started, let alone taken shape, without the enormous help and support of Becky Dobson. She spent hours with me to help shape the vaguest of memories into language that could be worked on. Her patience and good nature are legendary, and despite my uncouth behaviour and sharp manner we have developed a strong friendship, which I hope will endure the test of time. I have valued her input enormously.

A special thank you to Simon Phillips, whose advice and suggestions have been brilliant. His support in helping me find a publisher has been indispensable.

Anne Hill took on the unenviable task of bringing together everybody's contributions, as well as helping me with the writing of my own accounts. She managed to shape this account to become 'Ben Again', which I am extremely happy to have achieved with her support. I also want to say a huge thank you to all the other people who have made this book possible: Hugh Clench, Jenny Clench, Theo Clench, Naomi Clench, Alex Backenhouse, Robbie Barkell, Liz Beck, Caspar Chater, Diana Conyers, David Jackman, Andrew Jennings, Angie Konrad, Kellie Liket, Aoife McCullough, Caroline Radford-Weiss, Eduardo Ramos, Miles Raybould, Gideon Susman, Roland Susman, Yaz Talebian, Ross Tanner and Ali Walmsley.

Patrons List

Jan Alcoe
Paul Andrews
Greg Aradi
Christine Aubrey
Nicky Bagilhole
Emily Bailey
Susie Bartlett
Stephen Beecher
Jules Bevis
Marie Bismarck
Ella Blair
Sam Brhaspati
David Burnham
Suzy Butler
Aaron Butler
Katka Ceramics
Tania Cheung
Fran Connorton
Rebecca Craig
Anne Davison
Anita Devi
Chris Diplock
Jacky Dols
Helen Downes
Lauren Eva
Teresa Ferreiro
Fleur Finch
George Flatters
Fredrik Garpenfeldt
Kim Glass
Samantha Glover
James Gorridge
Tessa Grundon
Rona Gundry
Jean Haigh
Fiona Hall
Octavia Hamilton

Kate Hasson
Bet Hasson
Linda Hepper
Dot Hodgson
Bettina Horvat
Mike Hughesman
Julianna Hyjek
Merlin Iles-Jonas
Harriet JW
Tomas Kangro
Bridget Kindler
Angie Konrad
Claire Lazarus
Alex Lee
Sarah Lillywhite
Joanna Long
Yvonne Mangan
David Mason
John McElborough
Vivien Moore
Calum Morrison
Toby Penrhys-Evans
Georgina Powell-Stevens
Janet Pretty
Jennifer Riddington
Lisa Ross
Malgorzata Rynkowska
Jimmy & Yvonne Siu
Anne Stafford
Roland Susman
Sarah Susman
Hannah Swan
Yasmine Talebian
Jessica Thorpe
stephanie Vizer
Adam Wallace
Joel Walmsley
Gus Watcham
Noshua Watson
Alice White
Ian Williams

Pete Wrench
Alex Wright